For my husband, Luc ...
with all my food love

DELICIOUS
Every Day

anna gare

Contents

Introduction

I think that every day should be delicious. Life's just too short not to celebrate with moments and tastes that make you close your eyes and smile.

I live in the real world, though. I know that sometimes tyres go flat, but only when you're running late and wearing white; that work can feel like the wrong kind of Magic Pudding; and that even though we can send probes to Mars, I still can't fold a fitted sheet.

But with food, it can be delicious every day!

In writing this book I wanted to share with you the dishes I go to when I need a little delicious in my day. We've all got them: those trusted recipes we can knock out with one hand tied behind our back; those simple, yummy family favourites that don't leave you with a pile of dishes threatening to collapse the north side of your house.

I've been obsessed with food for a long, long time. As a toddler I made mud pies in the sandpit. It wasn't long before I graduated to the kitchen. My mum happily handed it over to me at a young age. She was no kitchen whiz and often blamed her stubborn old stove for her culinary disasters. When we finally got her a new one with self-ignition, she used it all the time ... as a cigarette lighter.

I consider myself lucky to have a mother who wasn't territorial about her kitchen because it became my playground and creative space.

Pretty soon I was cooking for the school canteen. Later, as a teenager touring in a rock band, I poached asparagus in hotel-room kettles and cooked salmon on the ironing board with waxed paper and the iron.

Since then I've run a catering business, cooked on TV, been a presenter at festivals and found myself championing some of Western Australia's greatest food regions — the Swan Valley and Margaret River, and my new home in the Great Southern region.

Over the years I have collected more than my share of delicious everyday meals. For this book I have narrowed them down to my hundred or so favourites.

Most of these recipes have been created by my desire to eat good healthy food that is preservative and additive free. Some are tweaks on dishes that my family has brought to Christmas lunches. Others have been inspired by those moments of bliss you experience at good restaurants or when someone else feeds you. And some of the best recipes are created from the only ingredients left in the fridge.

You'll find that there are recipes for every occasion and from just about every corner of the globe. I can't put borders around my taste so you'll find dishes in here inspired by Malaysia, Mexico, the Mediterranean and the Middle East, to name a few.

What they have in common is big flavours that make your tastebuds do a little interpretive dance, and a deep respect for good produce; plus they are full of colour and have that little extra something that makes you go back for more.

The techniques are simple and the guesswork has been taken out thanks to years of repetition in my kitchen. The ingredients are nutritious and usually easy to find, but if there are a few things you aren't familiar with, don't be scared, they can be found with just a little bit of looking. Believe me, your tastebuds will thank you for it.

Enjoy this book, and here's to making every day delicious.

Begin with BREKKIE

I like to believe that what you prepare for yourself and for others at breakfast is an expression of the day you intend to have. It can be the first act of kindness towards yourself with a green smoothie, or the fuel for a power-packed day with a herby scramble, quinoa and salmon bacon. If you are a dancer, then you will want something your body will respond to; if you're a yogi, then something a bit lighter and more balanced might do the trick. If you're going hang gliding, eat whatever you' want because it might be your last meal!

Bacon & egg frittata

The great thing about frittata at breakfast time is that you can colour it up with any leftover vegies from last night's dinner. Below is my delicious old-faithful version, guaranteed to set you up for a big day ahead or, perhaps, to help you recover from a big night before. Either way, it's a great way to start the day.

---

250 g (9 oz) rindless bacon slices

olive oil, for frying

1 garlic clove, finely chopped

4 spring onions (scallions), thinly sliced

10 eggs

200 ml (7 fl oz) thin (pouring) cream

2 teaspoons finely grated
   parmesan cheese

1 large handful of English spinach leaves

8 cherry tomatoes, halved

70 g (2½ oz) Danish feta cheese, crumbled

1 tablespoon pepitas (pumpkin seeds)
   and/or sunflower seeds

flat-leaf (Italian) parsley, to serve

PREHEAT the oven to 180°C (350°F).

DICE half the bacon slices finely and sauté in a 20 cm (8 inch) nonstick ovenproof frying pan with a dash of olive oil, until golden.

ADD the garlic and spring onions and fry for 1 minute to just soften.

WHISK 6 of the eggs in a bowl with the cream and parmesan and season with salt and pepper, then add the spinach leaves.

POUR the egg mixture into the pan with the bacon mixture and gently cook over medium heat without stirring for a few minutes.

REMOVE the pan from the heat, lay the remaining bacon rashers on top and crack in the remaining eggs. Scatter cherry tomatoes, feta and seeds over the top.

BAKE until the egg mixture is just firm and the eggs on top are still a little soft. Run a spatula around the side for easy release and then transfer onto a board or plate to serve, scattered with a few parsley leaves.

Bircher muesli *with* apple, strawberries & roasted hazelnuts

• SERVES 4 •

I love eating bircher muesli for breakfast as it makes me feel like I am indulging in a naughty treat! The first trick is soaking the oats overnight, as this gives them an extra creamy texture, but don't panic if you forget to do this before you go to bed — you can soak them for at least 15 minutes before serving and this will also work. With the addition of yoghurt, fresh fruit and crunchy nuts, you will realise that this is where healthy can taste nicely naughty, and this is definitely where nutritious food ticks all the boxes for me.

---

200 g (7 oz/2 cups) rolled (porridge) oats (not quick oats)

250 ml (9 fl oz/1 cup) apple juice (100% apple juice, not from concentrate)

130 g (4½ oz/½ cup) Greek-style yoghurt, plus extra for serving

1 large granny smith apple, grated

8 strawberries, hulled and halved

2 tablespoons roasted hazelnuts

a drizzle of honey, to serve

lemon juice, to serve

SOAK the oats overnight in a bowl with the apple juice (you can use water or milk instead).

ADD the yoghurt and grated apple and combine well.

SERVE in bowls with an extra dollop of yoghurt, topped with fresh berries and hazelnuts.

FINISH with a drizzle of honey and a squeeze of lemon juice.

Gluten-free crêpes & grilled pineapple *with* lime & orange syrup

• MAKES 12; SERVES 4 •

These days we all have a friend who can't eat dairy or wheat. Whether it's because they are following the latest fad or because their body simply can't tolerate those foods, it seems to be becoming the norm. I loved the challenge of creating a delicious crêpe recipe without the usual suspects and the result was perhaps even more deluxe.

---

500 ml (17 fl oz/2 cups) good-quality
    tinned coconut milk

4 eggs

2 tablespoons virgin coconut oil, melted

205 g ($7\frac{1}{4}$ oz/$1\frac{1}{4}$ cups) rice flour

45 g ($1\frac{1}{2}$ oz/$\frac{1}{4}$ cup) glutinous rice flour

1 small pineapple, peeled and cut into
    3 mm ($\frac{1}{8}$ inch) rounds

coconut cream or coconut yoghurt, to serve

LIME & ORANGE SYRUP

$2\frac{1}{2}$–3 tablespoons sugar

juice and finely grated zest of 2 limes

juice and finely grated zest of 2 oranges

WHISK the coconut milk, eggs, coconut oil and a pinch of salt in a bowl until combined.

SIFT in the combined rice flours slowly, whisking constantly until the batter is smooth.

STRAIN the crêpe batter through a sieve and set aside to rest for 1 hour while you make the lime and orange syrup.

HEAT the sugar and combined lime and orange juices in a small saucepan with 125 ml (4 fl oz/$\frac{1}{2}$ cup) of water and bring to the boil. Reduce heat and cook for about 10 minutes until it reduces by half and has a syrupy consistency.

ADD the lime and orange zests and simmer for a further 5 minutes. Remove from the heat and reheat when ready to serve. Taste once cooled slightly and adjust sweetness to your own liking.

GRILL the pineapple slices on a hot chargrill pan for 4 minutes on each side until scored and caramelised. Set aside and cover to keep warm.

LIGHTLY oil a nonstick pan, or crêpes pan and place over medium heat.

POUR 60 ml (2 fl oz/$\frac{1}{4}$ cup) of mixture into the pan, swirling in a circular motion to cover the base of the pan. Cook for 2–3 minutes until light golden. Turn over and cook for 1 minute.

TRANSFER to a plate and cover to keep warm. Repeat with remaining batter.

ARRANGE the crêpes and grilled pineapple on plates. Drizzle with the warmed lime and orange syrup and top with a spoonful of coconut cream or yoghurt.

Gluten-free muesli

MAKES ENOUGH TO FILL A 2 LITRE (70 FL OZ/8 CUP) JAR •

I love a healthy gluten-free muesli, but I find most ready-made versions really sweet and a bit light on all the good stuff. Take a quick trip to your local health-food store, where you will find a high turnover of fresh wholefood ingredients including local dried fruit and nuts. You can play around with the types of grains, fruit and nuts to suit your own taste.

---

45 g (1½ oz/¼ cup) sultanas (golden raisins)

80 g (2¾ oz) dried figs, finely chopped

80 g (2¾ oz) dried apricots, thinly sliced

80 g (2¾ oz) dried pear, finely chopped

60 g (2¼ oz) prunes, halved
  and thinly sliced

40 g (1½ oz/¼ cup) flaxseeds (linseeds)

40 g (1½ oz/1½ cups) puffed rice

100 g (3½ oz/1 cup) gluten-free rolled
  (porridge) oats

30 g (1 oz/1 cup) puffed quinoa or millet

30 g (1 oz/¼ cup) rice flakes

15 g (½ oz/¼ cup) flaked coconut

70 g (2½ oz/½ cup) lightly crushed
  macadamia nuts

40 g (1½ oz/¼ cup) pepitas (pumpkin seeds)

40 g (1½ oz/¼ cup) sunflower seeds

COMBINE all of the dried fruit and the flaxseeds together in a large bowl so the flaxseeds stick to the fruit and therefore won't fall to the bottom of the jar.

ADD the remaining ingredients, mix well and store in a big jar with a tight-fitting lid.

SERVE the muesli in a bowl with the juice of 1 orange and lashings of coconut or plain yoghurt.

16 DELICIOUS EVERY DAY

My very favourite smoothie

• MAKES 4 •

Green smoothies are all the rage at the moment and are a wonderful way to boost nutrition and energy levels for all the family. They have replaced the alarm clock in our house: it's the sound of the blender that lures the kids out of bed! This is my favourite combo.

2 large kale leaves, stems removed, roughly chopped

1 pear, seeds and stem removed, roughly chopped

1 apple, cored and roughly chopped

10 cm (4 inch) length of Lebanese (short) cucumber, roughly chopped

10 basil leaves

juice of 1 lemon

250 ml (9 fl oz/1 cup) water

2 cups ice

BLEND all of the ingredients in an upright blender until smooth.

POUR into glasses and serve immediately.

Herby scrambled eggs *on* quinoa *with* salmon bacon

• SERVES 2 •

Quinoa is often used in salads or served with a casserole to soak up the juices. It's famous for its nutritious qualities and a wonderful replacement for our trusty old friend toast at breakfast time. I like to serve a spoonful of quinoa with my scrambled eggs and top it with my latest obsession: smoked salmon fried until it's crispy and looks like bacon.

4 large eggs

125 g (4½ oz/½ cup) sour cream

1 handful of basil leaves, finely sliced

1 large handful of flat-leaf (Italian) parsley leaves, finely chopped

2 tablespoons chopped chives

4 slices smoked salmon

olive oil, for frying

4 large handfuls of English spinach leaves

1 tablespoon butter

200 g (7 oz/1 cup) mixed quinoa, cooked according to packet directions

WHISK the eggs and sour cream together in a bowl until combined.

STIR in the sliced and chopped herbs and season with salt and pepper.

FRY the salmon in a lightly oiled frying pan over medium heat for 1–2 minutes on each side until crispy. Set aside and keep warm.

ADD a dash more olive oil to the pan and toss the spinach over high heat for 1 minute, or until wilted.

MELT the butter in a nonstick frying pan over low heat and pour in the egg mixture.

USE a wooden spoon to gently fold the egg mixture in the pan.

REMOVE from the heat just before the egg mixture is set, as it will continue to cook.

SERVE on a bed of warm quinoa and top with the crispy salmon and wilted spinach.

Oat bran, quinoa & chia porridge

· SERVES 2–4 ·

It's not often we get three superfoods headlining at breakfast time. A humble bowl of porridge can be turned into a textural delight with the addition of quinoa and chia seeds. I love mine with almond milk as it makes it nutty and creamy, but if there's none in your pantry then coconut milk or regular milk will do the trick.

50 g (1$\frac{3}{4}$ oz/$\frac{1}{4}$ cup) white quinoa

100 g (3$\frac{1}{2}$ oz/$\frac{3}{4}$ cup) oat bran

1 tablespoon chia seeds

500 ml (17 fl oz/2 cups) water

500 ml (17 fl oz/2 cups) almond milk

3 tablespoons dried cranberries

TO SERVE

a drizzle of honey

2 tablespoons pistachio nuts

almond milk, extra

RINSE the quinoa in cold water and drain.

COMBINE all of the ingredients in a medium saucepan.

COOK gently over low heat, for 15–20 minutes, stirring occasionally until it thickens. It's important to cook it slowly so the quinoa cooks through.

SERVE topped with honey, pistachios and extra milk as desired.

Turkish baked eggs

• SERVES 4 •

You can't beat a tasty dish that only uses one pan. I dedicate this delicious recipe to all the people who do the dishes, and especially to my seven-foot-two hollow-legged husband, who, to his credit, has lowered all the benches in our kitchen just for me. He has, however, left the kitchen sink at 1.2 metres (47 inches).

2 tablespoons olive oil, plus extra,
    to serve
1 large brown onion, finely chopped
1 garlic clove, finely chopped
1 dried or fresh chorizo sausage,
    finely diced
1 teaspoon ground cumin
1 teaspoon smoked or regular paprika
$\frac{1}{4}$ teaspoon ground cinnamon
1 red capsicum (pepper), seeded
    and chopped
1 long red chilli, seeded and chopped
1 x 400 g (14 oz) tin chopped tomatoes
a pinch of sugar
4–6 eggs
130 g ($4\frac{1}{2}$ oz/$\frac{1}{2}$ cup) Greek-style yoghurt
$\frac{1}{2}$ lemon (optional)
flat-leaf (Italian) parsley leaves,
    to serve
Turkish bread, to serve

PREHEAT the oven to 200°C (400°F).

HEAT the olive oil in a 20–25 cm (8–10 inch) frying pan and gently fry the onion and garlic for a few minutes until soft.

ADD the chorizo, spices, capsicum and chilli and fry for a few more minutes, stirring so the spices don't burn.

ADD the tomatoes and 80 ml ($2\frac{1}{2}$ fl oz/$\frac{1}{3}$ cup) of water, and simmer over low heat for 15 minutes.

TASTE and season with salt, pepper and a pinch of sugar.

POUR evenly into four large ovenproof ramekins or keep in the pan if it is ovenproof.

MAKE indents in the sauce and crack in the eggs.

DOLLOP yoghurt randomly over the top.

BAKE in the oven for approximately 10 minutes, or until the egg whites have set.

SERVE with a squeeze of lemon juice (if using), extra olive oil, parsley and warm Turkish bread.

The lazy lady's loaf

I have a friend, Kareen, who says she can't cook and then rocks up with the most delicious home-made loaf of bread. I think the cleverest cooks are the ones who can turn something quite challenging into a simple triumph without any effort at all. This really is the cheekiest bread recipe I have ever made: I call it the lazy lady's loaf, not because you're lazy but because you can make it to perfection while you sleep.

---

500 g (1 lb 2 oz/3⅓ cups) unbleached plain (all-purpose) flour, plus extra for dusting and shaping

2 teaspoons instant yeast

2 teaspoons salt

475 ml (16 fl oz) lukewarm water

MIX the flour, yeast and salt together in a large bowl.

POUR in the water to make a sticky dough.

COMBINE with a spatula until well mixed.

COVER the bowl with plastic wrap and leave in the fridge overnight.

TAKE the dough out of the fridge the next day and rest at room temperature for about 1½–2 hours, depending on the weather (it must have just reached room temperature before you bake).

LINE a baking tray with baking paper and sprinkle generously with flour.

REMOVE the dough from the bowl using a spatula and put it on the prepared tray.

PRESS and shape the loaf into an oval ciabatta shape, using floured hands.

FLIP the loaf over so that the wrinkled, floured side is on top.

TRANSFER the tray to the cold oven and set the heat to 220°C (425°F).

BAKE for 45–50 minutes until the loaf is a light golden colour and sounds hollow when tapped.

COOL on a wire rack.

Haloumi *with* avocado mash, chorizo & cherry tomato salsa

For me, breakfast is not just about fuelling up for a busy day ahead, it's about enjoying an exciting combination of flavours and textures with a fresh palate. Haloumi has an extra endearing quality: when it's fried and you eat it, it squeaks!

2 avocados, halved and stone removed

juice of $\frac{1}{2}$ lemon

250 g (9 oz/1 punnet) cherry tomatoes, quartered

1 garlic clove, finely chopped

2 spring onions (scallions), thinly sliced

8 large basil leaves, thinly sliced

olive oil, for drizzling and frying

360 g (12$\frac{3}{4}$ oz) haloumi cheese, cut into 8 slices

1 dried or fresh chorizo sausage, thinly sliced diagonally

SCOOP out the flesh of the avocados and mash in a bowl with the lemon juice. Season with salt and pepper to taste.

TOSS the tomatoes, garlic, spring onions and basil together in a bowl, drizzle with olive oil and season with salt and pepper to taste.

HEAT some olive oil in a large nonstick frying pan and fry the haloumi for a few minutes on each side until golden and crispy. Remove from the pan and cover to keep warm.

ADD the sliced chorizo to the same pan and fry for 2 minutes on each side.

TO SERVE, lay the haloumi and chorizo slices on plates and top with the avocado mash and cherry tomato salsa.

NOTE: Haloumi is also delicious with crispy bacon if you don't have any chorizo.

Heartwarming Soups

There's a lot to love about soups: warm, nourishing, simple and healthy. They can be a labour of love or a quick, easy solution for a 6 o'clock dinner. They can be eaten over several days, added to, or frozen and reheated. Plus, it's very hard to make an unhealthy soup.

So my advice is to make a big potful and spend the week eating soup. Then you might just squeeze back into your favourite old jeans. Or, forgetting the old jeans, the great thing about soup as a meal is that it leaves room for dessert.

Green pea soup

• SERVES 4 •

**This is a great quickie if you have unexpected guests who rock up around lunch time.
I always have frozen peas in the freezer.**

---

2 tablespoons butter

1 large leek, white part only,
  finely chopped

1 brown onion, finely chopped

2 garlic cloves, finely chopped

1 litre (35 fl oz/4 cups) good-quality
  chicken or vegetable stock

700 g (1 lb 9 oz/5 cups) frozen peas

75 g ($2\frac{3}{4}$ oz/1 small bunch) dill, finely
  chopped, plus extra, to serve

130 g ($4\frac{1}{2}$ oz/$\frac{1}{2}$ cup) crème fraîche

HEAT the butter in a large saucepan over low heat. Add the leek, onion and garlic and cook for about 8 minutes until soft.

ADD the stock and bring it to boiling point, then reduce the heat and simmer for 10 minutes.

ADD the peas and cook for 3–5 minutes until they are tender.

REMOVE from the heat, season with salt and pepper and add the dill.

BLITZ the soup in an upright blender until smooth and creamy.

WHISK in the crème fraîche, scatter over some dill sprigs and serve.

TIP: Sometimes I use mint instead of dill; and if I don't have any crème fraîche, then yoghurt, cream or sour cream also work well.

Ham hock, vegetables & chickpeas

· SERVES 4–6 ·

We all love a delicious, hearty soup that's healthy and clean and leaves us feeling full but still energetic. This soup is very versatile and will work with any vegies you have on hand. I add chickpeas to my soup as they are a great source of soluble fibre, but cannellini beans or lentils can be delicious substitutes.

---

1 ham hock (or leftover ham bone)

2 litres (70 fl oz/8 cups) good-quality chicken or vegetable stock

1 brown onion, finely diced

3 garlic cloves, crushed

1 dried bay leaf

2 carrots, diced

3 celery stalks, diced

2 large potatoes, peeled and diced

1 x 400 g (14 oz) tin chickpeas (garbanzo beans), drained and rinsed

200 g (7 oz) green beans, sliced

1 zucchini (courgette), diced

1 small bunch of flat-leaf (Italian) parsley, finely chopped

PUT the ham hock in a large saucepan with the stock, onion, garlic and bay leaf and add 375 ml (13 fl oz/1½ cups) of water.

BRING to the boil then reduce the heat and simmer for 1 hour with the lid on. Allow to cool.

REMOVE the ham hock with a slotted spoon, discard the bone, skin and fatty bits, dice the lean meat and set aside. Skim any visible fat off the top of the stock with a spoon.

HEAT the stock to a simmer. Add the carrots, celery, potatoes and chickpeas and cook for 10–15 minutes.

ADD the beans, zucchini and diced ham and cook for a further 10 minutes, or until the zucchini and beans are tender.

SEASON with pepper, and salt if needed, keeping in mind that the ham is already quite salty!

SERVE in bowls, with the parsley sprinkled on top.

Lovely laksa *with* sweet potato noodles

· SERVES 4 ·

I love a good laksa and have no shame about cheating with a jar of quality paste. It's the most satisfying of soups, full of spice with pungent aromas. Often it is served with rice or egg noodles; however, having just purchased a fancy new spiraliser, I made some sweet potato noodles and they were a fantastic improvisation. You could use either.

400 g (14 oz) sweet potato, peeled and spiralised into noodles

1 tablespoon coconut oil

4 tablespoons good-quality laksa paste

500 ml (17 fl oz/2 cups) good-quality chicken stock

1 x 270 ml (9¼ fl oz) tin coconut cream

1 x 270 ml (9¼ fl oz) tin coconut milk

2 kaffir lime (makrut) leaves

1 tablespoon lime juice

1 tablespoon fish sauce

1 tablespoon grated palm sugar (jaggery)

400 g (14 oz) raw prawns, peeled and deveined, tails intact

3 bird's eye chillies, thinly sliced

100 g (3½ oz) deep-fried tofu or silken tofu, cut into cubes

130 g (4¾ oz) snow peas (mangetout), halved diagonally

200 g (7 oz) bean sprouts

1 large handful of coriander (cilantro) leaves

1 handful of Vietnamese mint leaves

1 handful of Thai basil leaves

2 tablespoons peanuts or fried shallots

STEAM the sweet potato noodles in a colander over a large saucepan of boiling water for 5–7 minutes until just tender but not breaking apart. Set aside and cover to keep warm until ready for serving.

HEAT the coconut oil in a wok or large frying pan over medium–high heat. Add the laksa paste and stir-fry for 2 minutes to bring out the flavours.

STIR in the stock and bring to the boil.

ADD the coconut cream, coconut milk and kaffir lime leaves.

REDUCE the heat to simmer for 5 minutes, then add the lime juice, fish sauce and palm sugar to taste.

ADD the prawns and cook for 3 minutes. Add the chillies, tofu and snow peas and cook for a further 2 minutes.

DIVIDE the sweet potato noodles among four serving bowls and evenly distribute the bean sprouts and fresh herbs.

POUR the laksa soup over the noodles, dividing the prawns equally among the bowls.

SCATTER with peanuts or fried shallots to serve.

Pork belly, pumpkin & black bean soup

• SERVES 4–6 •

Soups that fill you up and satisfy your soul are worth their weight in gold, and this is just one of those flavoursome dishes that makes you feel right at home. My son Jackson thinks this is the best soup in the world, so that makes me the best mum in the world when I make it for him.

2 tablespoons olive oil

2 leeks, halved lengthways
    and thinly sliced

4 garlic cloves, finely chopped

500 g (1 lb 2 oz) skinless pork belly strips,
    cut into 2 cm ($\frac{3}{4}$ inch) pieces

1 fresh chorizo sausage, diced

1 tablespoon fennel seeds

$\frac{1}{2}$ long red chilli, finely diced

1 tablespoon hot smoked paprika

2 litres (70 fl oz/8 cups) good-quality
    chicken stock

1 kg (2 lb 4 oz) butternut pumpkin
    (squash), peeled and cut into
    2 cm ($\frac{3}{4}$ inch) dice

2 x 400 g (14 oz) tins black beans,
    drained and rinsed

HEAT the oil in a large heavy-based saucepan over low heat and fry the leek and garlic lightly for a few minutes until soft.

ADD the pork, chorizo and fennel seeds and fry for 5 more minutes, or until the pork turns white. Stir occasionally to seal the pork and coat in flavours.

STIR in the chilli and paprika and add the stock.

BRING to the boil, then reduce the heat and simmer for 25 minutes.

ADD the pumpkin and simmer for a further 20 minutes, or until the pumpkin is just tender.

ADD the black beans for the last 5 minutes of cooking and season with salt and pepper to taste.

SERVE in big bowls.

Simple chicken & noodle soup

This is a fabulous quick soup if you have some leftover roast chicken. If you don't, you can always poach a chicken breast in the stock by simmering it gently for 10 to 15 minutes until cooked.

1.8 litres (63 fl oz) chicken stock

170 g (6 oz/¾ cup) small pasta,
   such as stellini or risoni

265 g (9⅜ oz/1½ cups)
   finely shredded chicken

310 g (11 oz/2 cups) peas

3 eggs

10 g (⅜ oz/⅓ cup) finely chopped
   flat-leaf (Italian) parsley

25 g (1 oz/¼ cup) grated parmesan cheese

20 g (¾ oz/1 small bunch) chives,
   finely chopped

freshly ground black pepper

HEAT stock to boiling point in a large saucepan.

ADD the pasta and cook according to the directions on the packet.

ADD the chicken and peas for the last 2 minutes of cooking time.

WHISK the eggs, parsley and parmesan together quickly in a bowl and then whisk the mixture into the hot stock. Cook for a further minute.

SERVE immediately, sprinkled with chives and pepper.

Cauliflower & celeriac soup

I like to serve this soup with grilled cheese on toast to make it a complete meal. Sometimes I serve it with a cheeky little scattering of blue cheese instead.

1 cauliflower

1 large brown onion, diced

1 leek, white part only, thinly sliced

4 garlic cloves, finely chopped

1 tablespoon butter

1 tablespoon olive oil

1 celeriac, peeled and chopped

1 teaspoon fennel seeds

1 dried bay leaf

2 vegetable or chicken stock
   (bouillon) cubes

250 ml (9 fl oz/1 cup) milk or thin
   (pouring) cream (optional)

salt and white pepper

PREPARE the cauliflower by removing the outer leaves and core. Cut the remaining stem and florets into small pieces.

FRY the onion, leek and garlic gently in the butter and oil over low heat for 8–10 minutes until soft.

ADD the celeriac, fennel seeds and bay leaf. Stir and cook for a further 5 minutes.

ADD the cauliflower, cover with water and crumble in the stock cubes.

BRING to the boil, then reduce the heat, cover with a lid and simmer for 30 minutes, or until the vegetables are tender.

DISCARD the bay leaf and blend the soup in a food processor or using a handheld blender until smooth. Add the milk or cream if you want a slightly thinner consistency.

SEASON to taste with salt and white pepper.

Spiced red lentil & coconut soup

· SERVES 6 ·

This soup has a wonderful creamy texture and is perfect for a wintry lunch or a light dinner.
I often serve it with fried roti, which I buy from the freezer section at my local Asian supermarket.

---

2 tablespoons coconut oil or vegetable oil

1 large brown onion, chopped

2 garlic cloves, chopped

1 lemongrass stem, white part only,
   chopped

1 tablespoon chopped fresh ginger

1 teaspoon ground turmeric

1 teaspoon ground cumin

1 teaspoon ground coriander

$\frac{1}{4}$ teaspoon ground cardamom

$\frac{1}{2}$ teaspoon ground cinnamon

$\frac{1}{2}$ teaspoon chopped dried red chilli

2 carrots, roughly chopped into
   2 cm ($\frac{3}{4}$ inch) dice

300 g (10$\frac{1}{2}$ oz) sweet potato, peeled
   and cut into 2 cm ($\frac{3}{4}$ inch) dice

1 large celery stalk, diced

305 g (10$\frac{3}{4}$ oz/1$\frac{1}{2}$ cups) dried red lentils,
   drained and rinsed

1 vegetable stock (bouillon) cube

1 x 270 ml (9$\frac{1}{2}$ fl oz) tin coconut milk

plain yoghurt, to serve

coriander (cilantro) leaves, to serve

lemon juice, to serve (optional)

HEAT the coconut oil in a large heavy-based saucepan over low heat. Add the onion, garlic, lemongrass and ginger, and gently sauté for about 8 minutes until soft and aromatic.

ADD all of the spices and sauté for a further 2 minutes.

STIR in the vegetables and lentils. Add 1.5 litres (52 fl oz/6 cups) of water and the stock cube and bring to the boil.

COVER with a lid, reduce the heat and cook for 20–30 minutes until the vegies are soft and the lentils are starting to break down. Remove from the heat.

BLITZ in the coconut milk using a handheld blender until the soup is smooth and creamy.

SERVE in lovely big bowls with small dots of yoghurt, fresh coriander leaves and a squeeze of lemon, if you like.

Ursula's Tuscan lentil & vegetable soup

• SERVES 4–6 •

Everything my friend and food stylist Ursula makes is delicious and this soup is no exception. She finely dices her ingredients to ensure that every spoonful is a harmonious medley of all the flavours.

180 g (6¼ oz) dried puy lentils

2 tablespoons olive oil

100 g (3½ oz) sliced pancetta, finely diced

3 garlic cloves, crushed

1 brown onion, finely diced

1 leek, white part only, finely diced

2 small carrots, finely diced

100 g (3½ oz) celeriac, finely diced

1 litre (35 fl oz/4 cups) good-quality
    chicken or vegetable stock

2 dried bay leaves

a few thyme sprigs

6 large curly kale leaves, stems removed,
    sliced and finely chopped (about 3 cups)

SOAK the lentils in plenty of water for a few hours or overnight.

RINSE the soaked lentils and simmer in fresh water for 10 minutes, then drain.

HEAT the olive oil in a large saucepan and lightly fry the pancetta over low heat until transparent.

ADD the garlic, onion, leek, carrots and celeriac and sauté for 10 minutes, or until fragrant.

ADD the drained lentils, stock, 1 litre (35 fl oz/4 cups) of water, bay leaves and thyme. Bring to the boil and simmer over low heat for 30–40 minutes, or until the lentils and vegies are tender.

TAKE out one big mug of the soup (with lots of lentils) and blend the cup contents in an upright blender (or use a handheld blender) until smooth, then add it back into the soup. This gives it a lovely texture and flavour.

ADD the chopped kale and simmer for 2 minutes.

TASTE and season with salt and pepper if desired, then serve.

Fresh fast pho

· SERVES 4–6 ·

The trick to a good pho is a fragrant stock. I cheat by buying a good-quality, preservative-free chicken stock and simply infuse it with lots of Vietnamese flavours. Traditionally this soup is served with julienned vegies and fresh herbs over rice noodles but I enjoy the slippery texture of rice paper.

STOCK INFUSION

1.8 litres (63 fl oz) good-quality
  chicken stock

3 cm (1¼ inch) piece of ginger,
  peeled and thinly sliced

½ long red chilli, sliced

3 teaspoons fish sauce

1 tablespoon salt-reduced soy sauce

1 tablespoon mirin (rice wine)

1 star anise

2 kaffir lime (makrut) leaves

1 lemongrass stem, white part only,
  cut into 3 pieces and bruised

1 teaspoon white sugar

PHO

1 small carrot, julienned

8 snow peas (mangetout), julienned

2 spring onions (scallions), julienned

115 g (4 oz/1 cup) bean sprouts

30 g (1 oz) enoki mushrooms, trimmed

1 long red chilli, thinly sliced

1 tablespoon julienned fresh ginger

8 sheets rice paper, roughly torn

100 g (3½ oz) silken tofu, sliced

1 large handful of coriander
  (cilantro) leaves

1 handful of Thai basil or
  Vietnamese mint leaves

MAKE the stock infusion. Put all of the ingredients into a medium saucepan. Bring to the boil, reduce the heat and simmer with the lid on for 45 minutes.

COMBINE all of the vegetables, chilli and ginger in a bowl and toss together gently.

DIVIDE the vegetable mixture evenly among serving bowls, layering with rice paper to ensure the paper doesn't stick together. Top with slices of tofu.

POUR the hot stock infusion over the top and scatter with the coriander and basil or mint leaves.

SERVE immediately.

NOTE: Finely shredded leftover cooked chicken or beef is also a great addition to this dish. Scatter the shredded meat over the vegetables with the tofu.

Finnish salmon soup

· SERVES 4 ·

My husband recently returned from a basketball trip to Finland. While he was there, he fell in love: luckily for me the object of his affection was a bowl of steaming Finnish salmon soup. I recreated this little number for him.

1 leek, white part only, finely diced

1 brown onion, finely diced

2 garlic cloves, finely chopped

2 tablespoons butter

550 g (1 lb 4 oz) potatoes, peeled and cut into 1.5 cm ($\frac{5}{8}$ inch) dice

1.5 litres (52 fl oz/6 cups) good-quality fish stock (sometimes I use half chicken stock and half fish stock)

2 dried bay leaves

a pinch of ground allspice

1 teaspoon freshly ground white pepper

100 ml ($3\frac{1}{2}$ fl oz) thin (pouring) cream

400 g (14 oz) salmon fillet, skinless, cut into 2 cm ($\frac{3}{4}$ inch) dice

100 g ($3\frac{1}{2}$ oz/1 large bunch) dill, finely chopped

2 spring onions (scallions), finely chopped

1 lemon, to serve

FRY the leek, onion and garlic gently in the butter over low heat for 10–15 minutes until soft and sweet.

ADD the potatoes, stock, bay leaves, allspice and pepper.

INCREASE the heat and bring to the boil.

REDUCE the heat to low and simmer for about 20 minutes until the potatoes are tender, but still holding their shape.

REMOVE a generous cup of the soup mixture with lots of potato in it and purée in an upright blender (or use a handheld blender) until smooth. Return the purée to the soup and stir in the cream.

ADD the salmon to the hot soup and season with salt and pepper. Remove from the heat and cover with a lid. Stand for 2 minutes.

STIR in the dill and spring onions.

SERVE immediately, with a squeeze of lemon.

Salads as the Main Attraction

On my long drives home to the country with my husband, the radio signal drops out and there is no mobile phone reception so we play the 'what if ...' game. I'm sure most couples have a version of this and those who do will know it can be a dangerous and dark game when played on the wrong topics. As a result I like to keep it light and breezy and on one of my favourite topics: FOOD!

WHAT IF ... you had to eat only one style of meal for the rest of your life? Of course my husband says meat — like any carnivorous hair-growing machine — but for me it's a no-brainer: the obvious answer is salad.

Salads are versatile; they can be healthy and light or indulgent and lavish. In this chapter I like to think I've catered for everyone, including my carnivorous, hairy husband. This is a collection of my latest salad obsessions, served as the main attraction of a light meal.

Vietnamese chicken salad

I always make this salad for lunch when I have leftover cold chicken. It's just so delicious and fresh and will fill you up without slowing you down. The trick to making this salad perfect is ensuring all the ingredients are thinly sliced. If you can't find Vietnamese mint you can use a combination of basil and mint or Thai basil.

½ cooked chicken, warm or cold

¼ small savoy cabbage, finely shredded

2 small carrots, julienned

¼ red onion, thinly sliced

large handful of Vietnamese mint leaves

1 handful of coriander (cilantro) leaves

175 g (6 oz/1½ cups) bean sprouts

1 Lebanese (short) cucumber, halved
   lengthways, seeded and thinly sliced

70 g (2½ oz/½ cup) crushed roasted peanuts

DRESSING

3 tablespoons lime juice

3 tablespoons fish sauce

2 tablespoons rice vinegar

1 tablespoon light brown sugar

1 red chilli, seeded and thinly sliced

1 teaspoon finely grated fresh ginger

SHAKE all of the dressing ingredients together in a jar and set aside to allow the flavours to develop while you make the salad.

PULL the chicken meat off the bones, discard any skin and shred the meat by tearing it with your fingers across the grain. Put the meat in a large bowl.

TOSS in all of the salad ingredients except the peanuts.

SHAKE the dressing again, taste for a good balance of flavours and adjust if needed, then drizzle over the salad.

SERVE in bowls or on a large platter, topped with a scattering of peanuts.

Warm squid salad

• SERVES 4 •

The great thing about squid is that it's a sustainable seafood, and it's also really quick to cook. It's extra-smoky when grilled on the barbecue and simply delicious tossed with a herby dressing while still warm.

---

600 g (1 lb 5 oz) whole cleaned baby squid

olive oil, for frying

DRESSING

125 ml (4 fl oz/½ cup) olive oil

125 ml (4 fl oz/½ cup) lemon juice

1 teaspoon salt

30 g (1 oz/1 cup) chopped flat-leaf (Italian) parsley leaves

2 tablespoons chopped dill

1½ tablespoons small salted capers, drained and rinsed

2–3 garlic cloves, finely chopped

2 long red chillies, sliced into rounds and seeds removed

1 teaspoon fennel seeds

COMBINE all of the dressing ingredients together in a bowl.

SLICE the squid tubes into 7 mm (¼ inch) thick rounds and leave the tentacles whole. Put the squid into a bowl.

DRIZZLE the squid with about 1 tablespoon of olive oil and season with salt and pepper.

FRY the squid on a piping hot barbecue or chargrill pan for about 2 minutes on each side. If you are using a small chargrill pan, do this in two batches so it doesn't stew.

TOSS in a bowl with the dressing and serve on a platter. It's delicious with crunchy bread and iceberg lettuce.

NOTE: If you are buying squid that hasn't been cleaned, you will need to purchase about 1 kg (2 lb 4 oz).

Goat's cheese brûlée salad

• FOR 2 TO SHARE •

There are various types of goat's cheeses suitable for this recipe. For the best result, purchase a round goat's cheese with a soft rind; when the cheese caramelises and melts, the rind holds it together, giving it a luscious, warm gooey centre. This is a great starter to share, or throw in a French bread stick and call it lunch!

2 baby beetroot (beets), red and yellow

1 tablespoon extra virgin olive oil

1 tablespoon sherry vinegar

1 teaspoon sweet raspberry vinegar

150 g (5½ oz) round of goat's cheese with soft rind (such as Saint-Secret Fromage de Chevre)

2 teaspoons caster (superfine) sugar

1 large handful of watercress

1–2 tablespoons walnuts, broken

1 small spring onion (scallion), white part only, julienned

baby rocket (optional)

STEAM the baby beetroot whole in a steamer over a saucepan of boiling water with the lid on for 20 minutes, or until they are just cooked through: they are ready when you can pierce them easily with a fork.

REFRESH under cold running water and use your fingers to rub off the skins.

CUT the beetroot into small wedges or cubes and dress with the olive oil, sherry vinegar and raspberry vinegar. Season with salt and pepper.

PREHEAT the grill (broiler) to high heat. Line a baking tray with baking paper and put the whole round of goat's cheese on it.

SPRINKLE the top of the cheese evenly with sugar. Grill for 8–10 minutes until golden and the sugar has caramelised.

PLACE the goat's cheese in the centre of a plate, surrounded by the beetroot (reserving dressing and juice).

ARRANGE the watercress, walnuts, spring onion and baby rocket (if using) around the plate, and drizzle over the reserved dressing.

Japanese beef salad

• SERVES 4 •

Sometimes we simply want a light summery dinner after a long hot day. These Japanese flavours are fresh, vibrant and totally satisfying. If you crave carbs then the addition of soba noodles will do the trick.

---

3 teaspoons white miso paste

1 teaspoon mirin (rice wine)

500 g (1 lb 2 oz) beef sirloin, trimmed of any fat, halved lengthways

200 g (7 oz) snow peas (mangetout), julienned

2 spring onions (scallions), thinly sliced diagonally

175 g (6 oz/1½ cups) bean sprouts, trimmed

½ telegraph (long) cucumber, halved lengthways, seeded and thinly sliced

1 small red capsicum (pepper), seeded and julienned

grapeseed oil, for cooking

200 g (7 oz) green salad leaves, such as tatsoi and mizuna

1 teaspoon black sesame seeds

DRESSING

3 tablespoons salt-reduced soy sauce

2 tablespoons grapeseed oil

¼ teaspoon sesame oil

1 tablespoon rice vinegar

1 tablespoon mirin (rice wine)

1 teaspoon grated fresh ginger

1 teaspoon light brown sugar

COMBINE the miso paste and mirin together in a bowl and rub this mixture all over the meat. Marinate at room temperature while you are preparing the salad.

SUBMERGE the prepared snow peas, spring onions, bean sprouts, cucumber and capsicum in a bowl of iced water until ready to assemble the salad (this makes it extra fresh and crunchy).

SHAKE all of the dressing ingredients together in a jar.

PREHEAT a barbecue or chargrill pan, drizzle with grapeseed oil and cook the sirloin over medium–high heat. Char for 4–5 minutes on each side until slightly blackened but still pink and rare on the inside.

REST, covered with foil, for 10 minutes, before thinly slicing 3–4 mm (⅛ inch) thick.

SPREAD the green salad leaves on a large platter or individual plates. Remove the vegetables from the iced water, drain and scatter two-thirds of the mixture over the leaves.

TOP with the sliced beef, scatter with the remaining vegetables, drizzle with the dressing and sprinkle with sesame seeds.

Fig & prosciutto salad *with* labneh & fennel-seed toffee

• PLATTER FOR 2 •

There are two things I love about summer time: the sun always shines and figs are in season. This salad has a deluxe combination of flavours and textures. You will need to strain the yoghurt in advance to make the labneh, but if you don't have time this recipe works well with marinated feta cheese or a soft goat's curd. The fennel-seed toffee really makes it extra special and is super-easy to make. This is a medium-set toffee and makes a little bit more than you need for the salad but I can guarantee that the leftovers will disappear quickly: it's really moreish. If you don't have agave syrup you can replace it with an extra tablespoon of raw sugar.

---

180 g ($6\frac{1}{4}$ oz) plain yoghurt

3–4 tablespoons broken fennel-seed toffee (see recipe below)

1 small red Asian shallot, peeled and thinly sliced

1 small Lebanese (short) cucumber, peeled, halved lengthways and thinly sliced

$\frac{1}{2}$ baby fennel bulb, thinly shaved

100 g ($3\frac{1}{2}$ oz) mixed salad leaves

1 handful of sunflower sprouts

4 thin slices of prosciutto, torn in half

3 large figs, quartered

2 tablespoons extra virgin olive oil

2 tablespoons sweet raspberry vinegar

1 handful of microgreens or soft herbs (optional)

STRAIN the yoghurt overnight in the fridge through a fine mesh sieve or muslin (cheesecloth) set over a bowl to catch the whey (liquid). Discard the whey (or you can drink it) and reserve the thickened labneh.

MAKE the fennel seed toffee (below). When it's cool, break it up into small pieces and set aside the quantity required for this salad. Store leftovers in an airtight container.

TOSS the shallot, cucumber, fennel, salad leaves and sunflower sprouts together gently in a bowl, then spread them out on a large flat platter.

ARRANGE the prosciutto and figs on top, then dollop on a few spoonfuls of labneh.

WHISK the olive oil and raspberry vinegar together, season with salt and pepper and drizzle generously over the salad.

SERVE topped with pieces of fennel-seed toffee and microgreens or soft herbs (if using).

FENNEL-SEED TOFFEE

1 tablespoon agave syrup

2 tablespoons raw (demerara) sugar

2 tablespoons water

1 teaspoon fennel seeds

$\frac{1}{2}$ teaspoon salt

1 tablespoon pepitas (pumpkin seeds)

1 tablespoon sunflower seeds

3 teaspoons toasted sesame seeds

2 teaspoons flaxseeds (linseeds)

FENNEL-SEED TOFFEE

LINE a baking tray with baking paper and set aside.

HEAT the agave syrup, sugar, water, fennel seeds and salt in a saucepan over low heat until the sugar dissolves and the mixture starts to boil.

INCREASE the heat to high. Do not stir; cook until the mixture turns a dark golden toffee colour.

REMOVE immediately from the heat, stir in remaining seeds and pour the toffee onto the prepared tray. Push the toffee with the back of a spoon to flatten it. Allow to cool and set.

Pomegranate chicken *with* fennel, feta & watermelon

• SERVES 4 •

Every ingredient in this salad is delicious in its own right, but when thrown together on a plate they sing and dance and carry on like a bunch of ladies on a girls' night out. This is a cool, fresh summery salad, easy to make and devour with friends.

---

2 plump skinless chicken breast fillets

2 tablespoons pomegranate molasses, plus extra, for serving

1 tablespoon grapeseed oil

$\frac{1}{2}$ small seedless watermelon, rind removed and cut into triangles

$\frac{1}{2}$ red onion, thinly sliced

$\frac{1}{2}$ fennel bulb, thinly shaved

extra virgin olive oil, for drizzling

1 lemon, halved, for squeezing

20 small mint leaves

180 g ($6\frac{1}{4}$ oz) Persian feta cheese, crumbled

1 small fresh pomegranate

PREHEAT the oven to 180°C (350°F). Line a baking tray with baking paper.

RUB the chicken breasts with the pomegranate molasses, grapeseed oil and some salt and pepper.

BAKE the chicken on the prepared tray, covered with foil, for 20–25 minutes until cooked all the way through. Allow to cool and slice thinly.

ARRANGE the watermelon, onion and fennel with the chicken on a large platter, drizzle with olive oil and squeeze lemon juice over.

SCATTER with mint leaves, crumbled feta and fresh pomegranate seeds. Put extra pomegranate molasses on the table for guests to drizzle over if they wish.

HOW TO PREPARE A POMEGRANATE
Cut 1 cm ($\frac{3}{8}$ inch) off the top and bottom of the pomegranate to expose the seeds and white pith. Slice down through the membrane to create 4–5 segments. Gently pry sections apart and turn each segment inside out over a bowl to catch the seeds. If some won't come out, gently tap the skin with a wooden spoon to help release the seeds. Discard any skin and white pith.

King prawn cocktail salad

I started working in restaurants back in the eighties when I was 15 years old. My first job in the kitchen was cooking, peeling and deveining the prawns. I did bucketloads daily. The prawn cocktail was served in a parfait glass, just as it had been in the seventies, and the punters loved it. Like a classic Andrew Lloyd Webber musical, a good dish never fades away and, thanks to evolution, it just gets better.

---

extra virgin olive oil, to dress salad

juice of 1 lemon, to dress salad

30 king prawns (shrimp), about 800 g (1 lb 12 oz), cooked, peeled and deveined, tails left intact

microgreens or sprouts (optional)

SALAD

150 g (5¼ oz) mixed salad leaves

3 red radishes, thinly sliced

200 g (7 oz) thin asparagus spears, trimmed and blanched

4 spring onions (scallions), thinly sliced

1 Lebanese (short) cucumber, thinly sliced

1 small baby fennel bulb, thinly shaved

1 avocado, stone removed, peeled and sliced

1 handful of dill, roughly chopped

DRESSING

60 g (2¼ oz/¼ cup) mayonnaise

65 g (2¼ oz/¼ cup) sour cream

70 g (2½ oz/¼ cup) plain yoghurt

2 teaspoons creamed horseradish (optional)

lemon juice, to taste

TOSS all of the salad ingredients together in a bowl and lightly dress with olive oil and lemon juice. Spread on a large serving platter.

COMBINE all of the dressing ingredients together in a bowl.

SCATTER the prawns over the salad and spoon the creamy dressing over.

SERVE garnished with microgreens or sprouts (if using).

HOW TO COOK PRAWNS: If frozen, thaw in the fridge overnight. Bring 2.5 litres (87 fl oz/10 cups) of water to the boil with a teaspoon of salt. Once rapidly boiling, add the prawns in two separate batches, cooking for 3–4 minutes each time until they rise to the top and float on the surface. Remove immediately with a slotted spoon and refresh in a large bowl of iced water for a few minutes to stop the cooking process. Remove the head and legs and peel off the shell, leaving the tail segment on. Make a small incision down the back of each prawn to devein. Store in the fridge until ready to serve.

Smoked trout & baby beetroot cake-tin salad

• SERVES 8 •

Moulding a salad in a cake tin is a creative way of preparing ahead of time and also has great wow factor!

---

350 g (12 oz) small beetroot (beets),
  a combination of red and yellow

extra virgin olive oil, to drizzle

2 teaspoons raspberry vinegar
  (or lemon juice)

650 g (1 lb 7 oz) kipfler potatoes, peeled
  and cut into 1 cm ($\frac{3}{8}$ inch) cubes

200 g (7 oz) stringless green beans,
  chopped into 1 cm ($\frac{3}{8}$ inch) pieces

2 tablespoons creamed horseradish

85 g (3 oz/$\frac{1}{3}$ cup) sour cream

85 g (3 oz/$\frac{1}{3}$ cup) mayonnaise

1 tablespoon baby capers

2 tablespoons chopped dill

3 spring onions (scallions), halved
  lengthways and thinly sliced

3 whole hot-smoked rainbow trout,
  skinned, deboned and flaked

sprigs of chervil or dill, for serving

STEAM the beetroot in a steamer over a saucepan of boiling water with the lid on for 20–30 minutes, until just soft. Using your fingers, peel the skin off under cold running water. Drain and cut into 1 cm ($\frac{3}{8}$ inch) cubes.

PUT the red and yellow beetroot in separate bowls so they don't discolour. Lightly drizzle over some olive oil and vinegar and season with salt. Set aside.

PREPARE the potatoes and beans. Put the potatoes in a large saucepan, cover with cold water and bring to the boil over high heat. Boil for 8–10 minutes until cooked through but still firm. Drain and cool slightly. Meanwhile, steam the beans in a colander placed over the potatoes for about 2 minutes. Refresh the beans in cold water. Drain and allow to cool.

COMBINE the horseradish, sour cream, mayonnaise, capers and dill in a large bowl and season with salt and pepper to taste. When the potatoes have cooled slightly, but are still warm, toss them in the horseradish mixture with the beans and spring onions.

ASSEMBLE by lightly greasing and lining the base and sides of a 20 cm (8 inch) diameter cake tin with plastic wrap, allowing extra wrap to overhang at the edge. This will be the cover once the tin is filled.

SCATTER the yellow and red beetroot cubes evenly to cover the base of the tin, then top with the flaked trout spread in an even layer.

SPOON the potato mixture over the trout, patting down gently with the back of the spoon to make it level.

ENCLOSE by folding over the overhanging plastic wrap and pressing gently to compact.

REFRIGERATE for 1 hour to set.

SERVE by removing the covering plastic wrap, placing a large flat plate over the cake tin and turning the salad out upside down. Remove the tin and plastic wrap. Garnish with fresh chervil and slice like a cake.

Salads to share

They say that sharing is caring, and I care when it comes to sharing a salad. It can reveal things about people. There are the horizontal grabbers who get all the crunchy, crispy and creamy bits off the top: they can be revealed as selfish or simply unaware. There are the pickers, who pretty much fall into the same category, and then there are the vertical-tong types who clearly have a well-developed sense of salad etiquette and a natural awareness of salad structure. Vertical pickers are welcome at my table and I have successfully trained all but one family member in the art (that one will always be a liability around a salad plate). Salad-sharing anxiety can easily be solved with a little tossing or layering, and by making sure all the ingredients you use are delicious!

Iceberg, pear & chive salad

Simple and crunchy, salty and sweet, with blue cheese dressing and rosemary croutons: this is a crowd pleaser.

---

1 tablespoon butter

1 rosemary sprig, leaves picked

12 wafer-thin slices of Turkish bread or ciabatta

1 iceberg lettuce, halved and cut into small wedges

2 pears, halved, cored and thinly sliced

25 g (1 oz/1 bunch) chives, cut into 2 cm ($\frac{3}{4}$ inch) lengths

1 heaped tablespoon mayonnaise

80 g (2$\frac{3}{4}$ oz) blue cheese, plus extra, crumbled, for serving (optional)

85 g (3 oz/$\frac{1}{3}$ cup) crème fraîche or sour cream

2–3 tablespoons lemon juice

PREHEAT the oven to 120°C (250°F).

MELT the butter in a small saucepan with the rosemary leaves and season with salt and pepper.

SPREAD the slices of bread out evenly on a baking tray and lightly brush with the melted butter.

BAKE for 10–15 minutes until the croutons are crunchy and light golden.

ARRANGE the iceberg lettuce and pear slices in a shallow bowl and scatter over the chives.

BLITZ the mayonnaise, blue cheese, crème fraîche and lemon juice together in a food processor until smooth and drizzle over the salad.

SERVE immediately, with extra blue cheese crumbled over, if desired.

Cauliflower salad

Cauliflower is having the time of its life. It spent the seventies and eighties covered in cheese, but now it's appearing on fancy restaurant menus as the star attraction. Here, it is teamed with tangy pomegranate to add sparkle and zing.

---

1 heaped teaspoon cumin seeds

1 heaped teaspoon coriander seeds

1 cauliflower, cut into small florets

2 teaspoons chopped garlic

1 teaspoon salt

freshly ground black pepper

3 tablespoons olive oil

3 spring onions (scallions), finely chopped

1 large handful of coriander
   (cilantro) leaves

1 handful of small mint leaves

$\frac{1}{2}$ pomegranate (see page 60 for tips on
   how to extract seeds)

1 tablespoon sunflower seeds

1 tablespoon pepitas (pumpkin seeds)

1 tablespoon toasted sesame seeds

DRESSING

3 tablespoons lemon juice

1 garlic clove, crushed

130 g ($4\frac{1}{2}$ oz/$\frac{1}{2}$ cup) Greek-style yoghurt

3 tablespoons tahini

1 teaspoon honey

PREHEAT the oven to 180°C (350°F).

TOAST the cumin and coriander seeds in a frying pan for 1–2 minutes. Finely grind the seeds using a mortar and pestle.

MIX the cauliflower florets in a bowl with the garlic, ground seeds, salt, pepper and olive oil.

ROAST the cauliflower on a large baking tray for 20 minutes, until lightly golden but still a little crunchy.

WHISK all of the dressing ingredients together and season to taste. Toss the cauliflower and spring onions in the dressing.

SPREAD half of the cauliflower mixture on a platter, scatter over half of the herbs, pomegranate seeds, and other seeds.

REPEAT with the remaining ingredients. Serve.

Greek goddess salad

• SERVES 6 AS A SIDE •

The traditional Greek salad is simple and delicious, and, when dolled up with a few extra lush ingredients, you can literally take her anywhere. She is happy at barbecues, picnics, feasts and quiet dinners at home. She has no boundaries and is often designed by what's in season or lurking around in the fridge. This is the way I like to dress her up for a party!

---

1 small fennel bulb, shaved

250 g (9 oz) mini cucumbers, sliced into thick rounds

400 g (14 oz) medley cherry tomatoes

1 yellow capsicum (pepper), seeded and cut into 2 cm ($\frac{3}{4}$ inch) squares

$\frac{1}{4}$ red (Spanish) onion, thinly sliced

1 large avocado, stone removed, peeled and cut into 2.5 cm (1 inch) pieces

150 g ($5\frac{1}{2}$ oz) green olives

2 tablespoons roughly chopped flat-leaf (Italian) parsley

2 tablespoons oregano leaves

150 g ($5\frac{1}{2}$ oz) marinated goat's feta cheese

DRESSING

1 tablespoon chopped dill

1 tablespoon fennel fronds

3 tablespoons lemon juice

1 large garlic clove, grated

1 teaspoon honey

3 tablespoons olive oil

MIX all of the salad ingredients, except the feta, together in a bowl.

SHAKE all of the dressing ingredients together in a jar with salt and pepper.

DRESS the salad in the bowl and toss gently.

SPREAD the salad on a serving platter and crumble the feta over the top.

Quinoa detox salad

Whenever I'm on a health kick this salad is a staple. Based on my favourite detox juice, it's just as delicious but so much more satisfying. Luckily my whole family enjoys it.

---

200 g (7 oz/1 cup) mixed quinoa

2 beetroot (beets), julienned

2 carrots, julienned

1 apple, julienned

2 spring onions (scallions), thinly sliced

1 large handful of mint leaves

30 g (1 oz/1 cup) roughly chopped
   flat-leaf (Italian) parsley

1 tablespoon chia seeds

DRESSING

2 teaspoons finely grated fresh ginger

2 teaspoons honey

3 tablespoons lemon juice

3 tablespoons olive oil

COOK the quinoa according to the packet directions. Alternatively, wash the quinoa in cold water and drain, then put it in a medium saucepan and add 500 ml (17 fl oz/2 cups) of cold water. Bring to the boil over high heat, then reduce the heat to medium–low and simmer for 10 minutes. Cover the saucepan with a lid, reduce the heat to low and cook for a further 5 minutes. Remove from the heat and stand with the lid on for 5 minutes. Fluff with a fork and allow to cool before adding it to the salad.

SHAKE all of the dressing ingredients with salt and pepper together in a jar. Set aside while you prepare the salad, to allow the flavours to develop.

COMBINE all of the salad ingredients, except the chia seeds, in a bowl, dress and toss.

SERVE on a platter, sprinkled with the chia seeds.

Green beans, broccolini & pancetta

• SERVES 4–6 AS A SIDE •

This recipe is an old faithful that graces our table as a perfect companion for roasted and barbecued meats.

---

250 g (9 oz) small French shallots, peeled

1 tablespoon olive oil

400 g (14 oz) green beans, trimmed

2 bunches of broccolini (tenderstem), cut in half, stems peeled and trimmed

12 slices of pancetta

1 teaspoon nigella (black onion seeds)

TARRAGON & MUSTARD DRESSING

1 teaspoon dijon mustard

3 tablespoons tarragon vinegar

125 ml (4 fl oz/½ cup) olive oil

1 garlic clove, crushed

2 teaspoons raw (demerara) sugar

1 teaspoon salt

freshly ground black pepper

PREHEAT the oven to 180°C (350°F). Line two baking trays with baking paper.

SPREAD the shallots on one prepared tray, drizzle with the olive oil and 2 tablespoons of water, then season with salt and pepper. Cover with foil and bake for 15 minutes.

REMOVE from the oven and turn the shallots over. Add another tablespoon of water if dry. Bake for a further 15 minutes, or until soft. Set aside to cool.

FILL a large saucepan halfway with water and bring it to the boil.

LAYER the remaining vegies in a steamer basket: first the beans, then the broccolini stems, then the broccolini flowers. Steam, covered, for 4 minutes over rapidly boiling water. Remove from the heat, refresh under cold water and allow to cool.

LAY the pancetta flat on the remaining prepared baking tray and bake for 5 minutes, or until crispy. Allow to cool on paper towel.

COMBINE all of the dressing ingredients together in a jar and shake until creamy.

TRANSFER the cooled vegies and pancetta to a bowl, pour the dressing over and toss to coat.

SERVE on a platter, sprinkled with the nigella seeds.

Raspberry pickled beetroot, labneh *and* hazelnuts

This salad has a wonderful combination of flavours and is totally delicious with just about anything. I first discovered sheep's milk labneh at the Albany Farmers' Market and have been addicted ever since. It can be hard to find in shops but is easily made by straining sheep's milk yoghurt overnight through a fine mesh sieve or some muslin (cheesecloth). This recipe also works beautifully with fresh goat's cheese.

---

125 ml (4 fl oz/$\frac{1}{2}$ cup) raspberry vinegar (unsweetened)

75 g (2$\frac{3}{4}$ oz/$\frac{1}{3}$ cup) caster (superfine) sugar

1 star anise

3 allspice seeds

2 beetroot (beets), peeled and thinly sliced (best done with a mandolin)

$\frac{1}{4}$ red onion, thinly sliced

80 g (2$\frac{3}{4}$ oz) baby rocket (arugula) leaves

extra virgin olive oil, for dressing

juice of 1 lemon

100 g (3$\frac{1}{2}$ oz) sheep's labneh

60 g (2$\frac{1}{4}$ oz) roasted hazelnuts

microgreens or soft herbs (optional)

PICKLE the beetroot by putting the vinegar and sugar in a 30 cm (12 inch) frying pan with 375 ml (13 fl oz/1$\frac{1}{2}$ cups) of water, the star anise and allspice and season with salt and pepper.

BRING to the boil, then reduce the heat.

ADD the sliced beetroot and cover with a lid or foil.

SIMMER gently for about 15 minutes, then cook uncovered for a further 15–20 minutes until the beetroot is tender and most of the liquid has been absorbed, leaving a residual thick syrup. Allow to cool.

TOSS the onion and rocket together and spread out on a serving platter.

COAT the beetroot in its residual syrup and scatter over the platter.

DRESS lightly with olive oil, lemon juice, salt and pepper.

DOLLOP teaspoonfuls of labneh randomly over the salad.

SCATTER with the hazelnuts and microgreens or soft herbs (if using).

NOTE: If you are making your own labneh, strain 200 g (7 oz) of sheep's milk yoghurt for at least 12 hours to result in about 100 g (3$\frac{1}{2}$ oz) of labneh.

Oven-dried tomato & eggplant dome

You can make this salad well in advance, even the day before; just bring it to room temperature before serving. If you have any leftovers, it makes a great filling for vegie lasagne or goes really well, reheated, with lamb.

---

12 firm, ripe roma (plum) tomatoes,
   halved lengthways

125 ml (4 fl oz/½ cup) olive oil, plus extra,
   for brushing and drizzling

3 teaspoons sugar, plus an extra pinch

sea salt and freshly ground black pepper

3 red onions, peeled

3 tablespoons balsamic vinegar, plus
   extra, for drizzling

2 eggplants (aubergines)

2 garlic cloves, crushed

a few thyme sprigs, leaves picked

1 handful of oregano or basil leaves

PREHEAT the oven to 100°C (210°F).

LAY the tomato halves, cut side up, on a large, rectangular ovenproof cooling rack. Lightly brush with olive oil and sprinkle with a pinch of sugar, sea salt and pepper. Stand the rack on a baking tray.

BAKE for 3 hours, or until semidried. Remove from the oven and set aside.

HEAT the oven to 180°C (350°F). Line two baking trays with baking paper.

CUT each onion into 6–8 wedges. Spread the wedges evenly on a prepared baking tray. Drizzle generously with 3 tablespoons of the olive oil and the balsamic vinegar. Sprinkle with 3 teaspoons of sugar and some sea salt and pepper.

CUT the eggplants in half lengthways, then cut each half into 6–8 wedges.

MIX 3 tablespoons of the olive oil with the garlic and some pepper and sea salt. Brush the mixture on both sides of each wedge and lay them flat on the remaining baking tray.

BAKE both trays of vegetables for about 25 minutes, turning the wedges over halfway through the cooking time. The eggplant should be golden and still holding its shape.

ALLOW to cool completely before moulding.

MOULD the salad by lining a 2-litre (70 fl oz/8 cup) stainless-steel bowl with plastic wrap.

COVER the base and side of the bowl with some of the roasted eggplants, tomatoes and onions. Make it look pretty.

COMBINE the remaining roasted vegies and fresh herbs in a separate bowl. Drizzle with the remaining olive oil and balsamic vinegar, tossing gently.

SPOON the mixture into the centre of the lined bowl. Cover with plastic wrap and press down gently. Allow to rest in fridge for at least 30 minutes.

UNMOULD by turning the salad upside down onto a large platter, and serve.

DELICIOUS with an extra drizzle of olive oil and some fresh herbs sprinkled on top.

Simple SIDES

Someone who has their own sense of style can turn a basic black frock into a fashion statement with a simple accessory. They can make jeans and a jacket look chic with a scarf. Even a pair of sunglasses can do the trick.

Most people are pretty confident grilling a steak, roasting a chicken or pan-frying some fish. But think about dressing things up with some of my simple sides because food, like fashion, can be taken to another level with the right accessories.

The dishes in this chapter can make your basic black-frock dish look good in any situation, and will occasionally solve a meal riddle all by themselves.

Greek potatoes

· SERVES 4–6 ·

Every Christmas my family chooses a menu theme, we all bring a dish and everyone goes
to a LOT of trouble. Last year my bro-in-law Sam — to my surprise — rocked up super-relaxed
with a tray of 'baked potatoes'. Little did I know they would steal the show. Needless to say,
I have stolen his recipe.

1.2 kg (2 lb 10 oz) potatoes, peeled and cut
    into 3–4 cm ($1\frac{1}{4}$–$1\frac{1}{2}$ inch) pieces
60 ml (2 fl oz/$\frac{1}{4}$ cup) olive oil
125 ml (4 fl oz/$\frac{1}{2}$ cup) lemon juice
250 ml (9 fl oz/1 cup) chicken stock
4 garlic cloves, finely chopped
1 teaspoon dried Greek oregano
1 teaspoon sea salt
freshly ground white pepper
2 tablespoons chopped oregano leaves
2 tablespoons chopped flat-leaf (Italian)
    parsley leaves

PREHEAT the oven to 200°C (400°F).

SPREAD the potatoes out in a medium roasting tin.

MIX the olive oil, lemon juice, stock, garlic, dried oregano,
salt and pepper in a bowl. Pour over the potatoes.

COVER tightly with foil and bake for 50 minutes, or until
the potatoes are just soft.

REMOVE the foil, sprinkle with the chopped oregano and toss.
Bake for a further 20 minutes, or until slightly golden.

SERVE hot, sprinkled with the parsley.

Herby couscous & chickpeas

• SERVES 4 •

A great side serving for saucy dishes like tagines and casseroles. Any leftovers will make a nice salad the next day jazzed up with some roast vegies or meat. It keeps for a few days in the fridge and is best reheated in the microwave.

190 g (6¾ oz/1 cup) couscous

boiling water, to just cover couscous

2 red onions, finely chopped

2 garlic cloves, crushed

3 tablespoons olive oil

50 g (1¾ oz/½ cup) flaked almonds, roasted

2 tablespoons chopped preserved lemon

1 x 400 g (14 oz) tin chickpeas, drained
   and rinsed

1 large handful of flat-leaf (Italian)
   parsley leaves

1 large handful of mint leaves

1 large handful of coriander
   (cilantro) leaves

POUR the couscous into a large bowl, add boiling water to cover by about 5 mm (¼ inch), cover with a plate and allow to stand for 5 minutes while the couscous absorbs the water.

FRY the onion and garlic in the oil over medium heat until soft.

ADD the almonds, preserved lemon and chickpeas and sauté for 2 minutes to heat through.

FOLD the cooked mixture into the couscous.

CHOP the herbs and fold them through the couscous mixture.

SEASON with salt and pepper and serve.

Persian rice & lentil bake

· SERVES 4–6 ·

This is an aromatic way to cook rice and lentils together. If you have left it too late to presoak the lentils and wild rice you can precook them for 20 minutes, then drain well before adding to the basmati rice.

---

105 g ($3\frac{5}{8}$ oz/$\frac{1}{2}$ cup) puy lentils

3 tablespoons wild rice

750 ml (26 fl oz/3 cups) hot chicken
    or vegetable stock

a pinch of saffron threads

3 tablespoons olive oil

1 large brown onion, finely chopped

1 teaspoon ground cumin

1 teaspoon ground coriander

$\frac{1}{4}$ teaspoon ground turmeric

$\frac{1}{2}$ teaspoon ground cardamom

$\frac{1}{2}$ teaspoon ground cinnamon

$\frac{1}{4}$ teaspoon ground cloves

200 g (7 oz/1 cup) basmati rice

35 g ($1\frac{1}{4}$ oz/$\frac{1}{4}$ cup) pistachio nuts

35 g ($1\frac{1}{4}$ oz/$\frac{1}{4}$ cup) slivered almonds

55 g (2 oz/$\frac{1}{3}$ cup) dried cranberries

75 g ($2\frac{3}{4}$ oz/$\frac{1}{2}$ cup) currants

a few coriander (cilantro) sprigs,
    to garnish

SOAK the lentils and wild rice in cold water for 2 hours, then strain in a colander.

PREHEAT the oven to 180°C (350°F).

HEAT the stock in a saucepan with the saffron.

HEAT the olive oil in a 30 cm (12 inch) ovenproof frying pan and gently fry the onion until translucent.

ADD the spices and gently fry for 2 minutes.

ADD the strained lentils, wild rice and the basmati rice.

INCREASE the heat to medium–high and stir continuously for 3 minutes to coat the rice in spices.

ADD the nuts and dried fruit and stir over the heat for another 2 minutes.

POUR the boiling stock into the pan, stir to combine and then level the mixture out.

COVER the pan with baking paper and a well-fitting lid (or use foil). Transfer immediately to the oven.

BAKE for 30 minutes, or until the rice is cooked and the stock is completely absorbed. Remove from the oven and stand for a further 5 minutes, covered.

TO SERVE, fluff up the rice and lentils with a fork and scatter over the coriander leaves.

Warm steamed baby vegies
with tarragon aïoli

• SERVES 4–6 •

Steamed baby veg makes a lovely side dish and, when served with a creamy aïoli, it's even lovelier.

---

350 g (12 oz/1 bunch) baby carrots, peeled

6 baby zucchini (courgettes), halved

6 yellow baby (patty pan) squash, quartered

150 g (5½ oz) sugar snap peas, strings removed

175 g (6 oz/1 bunch) baby asparagus

juice of ½ lemon

extra virgin olive oil, to drizzle

FIRST make the tarragon aïoli (see recipe below).

BRING a large saucepan half-full of water to the boil.

SET a large colander over the top of the saucepan and add the carrots. Cover with a lid and steam for 4 minutes.

PUT the zucchini and squash on top of the carrots, re-cover and cook for a further 3 minutes.

ADD the sugar snap peas and asparagus, re-cover and cook for a further 2 minutes. Remove from the heat and drain.

TOSS the vegies in a bowl with salt and pepper, the lemon juice and a drizzle of olive oil.

SERVE the vegies on a large platter, dressed with tarragon aïoli.

TARRAGON AÏOLI

2 egg yolks

1 teaspoon dijon mustard

2 garlic cloves, crushed

100 ml (3½ fl oz) olive oil

50 ml (1¾ fl oz) tarragon vinegar

lemon juice

TARRAGON AÏOLI

BEAT the egg yolks, mustard and garlic together until creamy.

WHISK in the olive oil, adding it in a thin stream until it is all incorporated, then whisk in the vinegar.

ADD lemon juice to taste, then season with salt and pepper.

DELICIOUS with the steamed vegies (above), or with grilled and roasted fish or meats.

Baked vegies *with* garlic

• SERVES 4–6 •

This is my quick go-to vegetable fix that makes a great accompaniment for just about anything. It's truly delicious with lamb chops.

---

1 large fennel bulb, cut into 8 wedges

2 small red onions, cut into 6 wedges

1 small red capsicum (pepper), seeded and cut into 6 strips

1 small yellow capsicum (pepper), seeded and cut into 6 strips

2 zucchini (courgettes), cut into 3 cm (1¼ inch) rounds

2 garlic bulbs, halved across

a few thyme sprigs

2 teaspoons sugar

3 tablespoons olive oil

3 tablespoons verjuice

PREHEAT the oven to 180°C (350°F).

SPREAD the vegies, garlic and thyme on a baking tray lined with baking paper.

SPRINKLE the sugar, olive oil and verjuice evenly over the top and season with salt.

BAKE for 40–50 minutes, or until the vegies are tender.

NOTE: If you don't have verjuice, you can use a splash of wine, white wine vinegar or lemon juice.

Broccolini, almonds, chilli, garlic & lemon

· SERVES 4–6 ·

Broccolini is the pretty hybrid cousin of broccoli and Chinese kale. Its slender broccoli florets are long, with sweet tender stalks, and it makes an absolutely gorgeous simple side dish when lightly steamed and then stir-fried with some robust flavours.

2–3 bunches of broccolini (tenderstem)

2 tablespoons olive oil, plus extra
  to drizzle

2 garlic cloves, finely chopped

1 red chilli, finely chopped

zest and juice of 1 lemon

sea salt and freshly ground black pepper

2 tablespoons roasted flaked almonds
  (optional)

TRIM 1 cm ($\frac{3}{8}$ inch) off the end of each broccolini stem and peel the skin off the remaining stems with a potato peeler. This will make them nice and tender when cooked.

STEAM, covered, in a colander over a saucepan of boiling water for 2 minutes.

HEAT the olive oil in a medium frying pan and lightly fry the garlic and chilli for 1–2 minutes until soft.

ADD the lemon zest and steamed broccolini. Increase the heat and toss for 1 minute to coat with the flavours.

SQUEEZE lemon juice over the pan and season with salt and pepper. Cook for a further minute.

REMOVE from the heat, drizzle with the extra olive oil and scatter with roasted flaked almonds (if using).

SERVE immediately on a platter or in the pan.

Honey baked carrots *with* caraway seeds

· SERVES 4–8 ·

**I use a combo of purple and orange carrots to make this more colourful.
Delicious with Persian spiced lamb racks (see page 112).**

800 g (1 lb 12 oz/2–3 bunches)
   baby carrots, trimmed
2 tablespoons olive oil
1 tablespoon honey
½ teaspoon caraway seeds

PREHEAT the oven to 200°C (400°F).

WASH the carrots and transfer them to a large ovenproof dish without drying them. The residual water on the carrots will help speed up the cooking process.

TOSS the remaining ingredients together with the carrots to season.

BAKE for 20 minutes covered with foil, then remove the foil and bake for a further 20 minutes uncovered.

Caramelised fennel

· SERVES 4 ·

Fennel is my favourite vegetable. Unlike with children, you can admit to having one you prefer.

2 plump fennel bulbs, cut into 8 wedges,
   keeping base intact
1 garlic clove, finely chopped
1 teaspoon fennel seeds
3 bay leaves
2 teaspoons sugar
125 ml (4 fl oz/½ cup) chicken or
   vegetable stock
3 tablespoons verjuice
2 tablespoons olive oil

PREHEAT the oven to 180°C (350°F).

SPREAD the fennel wedges on a lightly oiled nonstick baking tray (or line the tray with baking paper).

MIX the remaining ingredients together in a bowl, season with salt and pepper and pour over the fennel.

COVER with foil and bake for 30–40 minutes until tender.

REMOVE the foil and turn the fennel over. Bake for a further 10–20 minutes uncovered until they are golden and caramelised.

Kale, pine nuts, lemon & feta

• SERVES 4–6 •

Kale has made a comeback over the last few years, becoming the talk of the town and the superfood listed on every healthy-eating celebrity's top ten. Like most of the cabbage (brassica) family, slugs and snails also find it delicious, therefore commercial kale crops are often sprayed with pesticides. The good news is, it's super-easy to grow yourself. If buying from the shops, choose organic and just wash the leaves really well. This is a really yummy and easy recipe that I think everyone should have in their repertoire.

---

1 bunch curly kale, stems removed

2 tablespoons olive oil

2 garlic cloves, finely chopped

juice of $\frac{1}{2}$ lemon

60 g ($2\frac{1}{4}$ oz) feta cheese, crumbled

40 g ($1\frac{1}{2}$ oz/$\frac{1}{4}$ cup) pine nuts, toasted

WASH, drain and finely shred the kale leaves.

HEAT the olive oil in a large frying pan over low heat and fry the garlic for 1 minute, or until lightly golden; be careful not to let it burn.

ADD the kale and toss over high heat for about 2 minutes until wilted.

SQUEEZE lemon juice over and season with salt and pepper.

TRANSFER immediately to a platter, scatter with the crumbled feta and pine nuts, and serve.

Quick WEEK-NIGHT MEALS

In this chapter I have included my favourite quick weeknight dishes for people on the run, under pressure or simply without time for too much planning and fuss. I can guarantee that any one of these recipes will provide hungry family members with delicious sustenance on evenings when time and inspiration are in short supply.

Crumbed pork loin *with* winter slaw

• SERVES 4 •

Pork and slaw have the perfect marriage, often paired on menus because the mild flavour of the pork goes nicely with a fruity and fresh crunchy slaw. I've gently heated the slaw and added caraway, mustard seeds and verjuice — it has really livened things up.

400 g (14 oz) pork sirloin or scotch
   fillet steaks

1 egg, lightly beaten

3 tablespoons milk

50 g ($1\frac{3}{4}$ oz/$\frac{1}{3}$ cup) plain (all-purpose) flour

105 g ($3\frac{5}{8}$ oz/$1\frac{3}{4}$ cups) panko breadcrumbs

3 tablespoons olive oil

2 tablespoons butter

125 g ($4\frac{1}{2}$ oz/$\frac{1}{2}$ cup) crème fraîche mixed
   with 1 tablespoon dijon mustard,
   to serve

PREPARE the pork by laying it between two sheets of plastic wrap and flattening it with a meat mallet until it is about 5 mm ($\frac{1}{4}$ inch) thick.

WHISK together the egg and milk with some salt and pepper in a bowl.

SPREAD the flour and breadcrumbs out evenly on two separate trays. Season lightly with salt and pepper.

COAT the pork in flour and shake to remove any excess.

DIP the pork into the egg mixture and then press into the breadcrumbs. Pat the breadcrumbs onto the meat until both sides are evenly coated.

HEAT the olive oil and butter in a large frying pan and cook the schnitzel over medium to low heat, for 5–6 minutes on each side until golden and cooked through.

SERVE with winter slaw (see recipe below) and the mustard crème fraîche in a bowl.

WINTER SLAW

$\frac{1}{2}$ small savoy cabbage, finely shredded

1 small fennel bulb, halved and
   thinly sliced

1 granny smith apple, quartered,
   cored and thinly sliced

2 tablespoons olive oil

1 large garlic clove, finely chopped

1 large red onion, halved and thinly sliced

1 teaspoon black mustard seeds

2 teaspoons caraway seeds

3–4 tablespoons verjuice

1 handful of flat-leaf (Italian) parsley,
   leaves picked

WINTER SLAW

COMBINE the cabbage, fennel and apple in a bowl.

HEAT the olive oil in a large frying pan or wok over medium heat. Add the garlic, onion, mustard seeds and caraway seeds and fry for 2 minutes, or until the onion softens and the mustard seeds start to pop.

ADD the cabbage mixture to the pan, increase the heat and cook for 5 minutes, tossing to heat through and wilt the cabbage.

ADD the verjuice and parsley. Cook for a further minute, then season with salt and pepper and serve.

Paprika steak *with* coriander relish

There's nothing like a quick grilled steak for dinner. Dressed up in a smoky paprika marinade with salty preserved lemon, it's in my top ten favourite weeknight dinners. This marinade also works really well with squid and other seafood, as does the fresh coriander relish.

4 x 200–250 g (7–9 oz) scotch fillet steaks, about 3 cm (1¼ inches) thick

MARINADE

2 teaspoons smoked paprika

1 tablespoon finely chopped garlic

1 tablespoon finely chopped preserved lemon

2–3 tablespoons olive oil

CORIANDER RELISH

120 g (4¼ oz/4 cups) coriander (cilantro) leaves, roughly chopped

1 long green or red chilli, roughly chopped

1 large garlic clove, roughly chopped

1 teaspoon sugar

½ teaspoon sea salt

3 tablespoons lemon juice

3 tablespoons extra virgin olive oil

COMBINE all of the marinade ingredients in a bowl and coat the steaks in the marinade. Leave them to stand in the marinade for half an hour to bring them to room temperature.

POUND the coriander, chilli, garlic, sugar and salt for the relish to a paste using a mortar and pestle (or use a food processor), then stir in the lemon juice and olive oil.

COOK the steaks on a hot barbecue or chargrill pan for about 8 minutes on each side for medium rare, or until done to your liking.

SERVE with the coriander relish.

DELICIOUS with baked vegies with garlic (see page 93), roasted carrots or a simple salad.

Broccoli pasta

It's hard to imagine that you can conjure up a beautiful meal for the whole family based on one head of broccoli. Dress it up with pungent flavours and the broccoli comes to life.

---

1 head of broccoli, including
    stalks and leaves

375 g (13 oz) spaghetti

3 tablespoons olive oil

4 large garlic cloves, finely chopped

2 long red chillies, finely chopped

8 anchovies, finely chopped

2 tablespoons pine nuts (optional)

50 g ($1\frac{3}{4}$ oz/$\frac{1}{2}$ cup) finely grated
    parmesan cheese

zest of 1 lemon, finely grated with
    a microplane

2 large handfuls of flat-leaf (Italian)
    parsley leaves, finely chopped

WASH and drain the broccoli. Remove the big outer leaves and discard. Set aside the smaller, tender leaves. Cut the broccoli into small florets. Peel the tough outer skin from the stalk until you get to the white core. Cut this into 5 mm ($\frac{1}{4}$ inch) cubes.

COOK the spaghetti in a large saucepan of boiling salted water according to the packet directions.

MEANWHILE, steam the broccoli in a colander over the boiling pasta (put the diced stalks on the bottom, then the florets, then leaves) for 4 minutes, or until just tender. Drain and set aside.

HEAT the olive oil in a wok or large, deep sauté pan and fry the garlic, chilli, anchovies and pine nuts over low heat for 2–3 minutes until just turning golden. Be careful not to burn the mixture.

INCREASE the heat and add the steamed broccoli and 125 ml (4 fl oz/$\frac{1}{2}$ cup) of the pasta cooking water to the frying pan and cook for a further 2 minutes.

DRAIN the pasta and add it to the broccoli mixture.

ADD the parmesan, lemon zest and parsley. Season with salt and pepper.

TOSS together and serve.

Pork fillet, parsnip purée, buttery spinach & peas

This is my hot-favourite dinner right now. It graces our table on an almost weekly basis and no-one complains.

---

380 g (13½ oz) parsnips, peeled
  and cut into 1 cm (⅜ inch) dice
2 garlic cloves, finely chopped
375 ml (13 fl oz/1½ cups) milk
salt and white pepper
600 g (1 lb 5 oz) pork fillet, trimmed
  of any sinew
1 tablespoon olive oil, plus extra for frying
3 sage leaves, finely chopped
3 tablespoons verjuice
2 tablespoons butter
250 g (9 oz) English spinach, stems
  trimmed
140 g (5 oz/1 cup) frozen peas,
  rinsed and thawed

PREHEAT the oven to 200°C (400°F).

PUT the diced parsnips, 1 garlic clove, milk, salt and white pepper into a saucepan and bring to the boil. Reduce the heat, cover with a lid, and simmer for 20 minutes, or until the parsnips are tender.

STRAIN the parsnips, reserving 125 ml (4 fl oz/½ cup) of the cooking liquid.

BLITZ the parsnips in a food processor until creamy, adding small amounts of the reserved cooking liquid to make a smooth purée consistency. Add more or less depending on how thick you like it.

SEASON the pork fillet in a bowl with salt and pepper, the olive oil and sage. If one end is thin, tuck it under and tie with kitchen string to ensure even cooking.

HEAT the extra olive oil in an ovenproof frying pan over medium–high heat. Add the pork fillet and cook for 2 minutes, or until lightly browned all over.

TRANSFER to the oven and bake for 15–20 minutes, depending on the thickness of the fillet. Test the thickest part with a skewer to see if the juices run clear.

REST on a plate, covered in foil, for 5 minutes: perfect timing to cook the spinach and peas.

DEGLAZE the pan over high heat with 2 tablespoons of the verjuice. Cook for 1 minute and then pour the pan juices over the resting meat and re-cover with foil.

HEAT the butter in the same pan with the remaining garlic and gently sauté until the garlic is soft.

ADD the spinach and peas and sauté for 2–3 minutes, then add the remaining verjuice and cook for a further minute, or until the spinach is wilted and the peas are heated through.

TO SERVE, slice the pork into medallions. Spoon the parsnip purée onto plates, top with the spinach and peas, pork medallions and drizzle with any remaining juices.

Zucchini noodles *with* herby cherry tomatoes, lemon & feta

If wheat-based pasta leaves you feeling bloated and tired, improvise with zucchini noodles instead. I recently made this for my family to change things up and now it's our preferred option. (You can make the noodles with a sharp potato peeler and knife but I highly recommend investing in a spiral vegetable cutter.)

---

3 zucchini (courgettes), about 750 g (1 lb 10 oz)

3 tablespoons olive oil

4–5 garlic cloves, finely chopped

700 g (1 lb 9 oz) medley cherry tomatoes, halved

zest and juice of $\frac{1}{2}$ lemon

1 handful of flat-leaf (Italian) parsley leaves, chopped

1 handful of dill, chopped

1 handful of sweet marjoram leaves, chopped

20 g ($\frac{3}{4}$ oz/1 small bunch) chives, finely chopped

120 g ($4\frac{1}{4}$ oz) Greek feta cheese, crumbled

CUT the zucchini into manageable pieces for a spiral vegetable cutter. Make noodles according to the manufacturer's instructions.

BRING a large saucepan half-full of water to the boil.

SET a large colander over the top of the boiling water, put in the zucchini noodles, cover with a well-fitting lid and steam for 5–7 minutes until al dente. Don't overcook the noodles or they will lose their shape and break.

MEANWHILE heat the oil in a large frying pan over low heat.

GENTLY fry the garlic for 1 minute, or until soft.

TOSS in the tomatoes, increase the heat to high and cook for 3 minutes, stirring occasionally to ensure even cooking.

ADD the lemon zest and juice, the herbs and season with salt and pepper. Cook for a further 3 minutes, or until the tomatoes blister and are heated through.

STRAIN the zucchini noodles, as they retain water.

SERVE the herby tomatoes over the zucchini noodles, topped with the crumbled feta.

Cevapcici *with* ajvar relish

• MAKES 14 •

I used to buy cevaps from my local Croatian butcher, but sadly — like many good butchers — he closed down years ago, so now I make my own. They are really yummy served with the traditional ajvar (roasted capsicum and eggplant) relish. You can buy ajvar in the international section of the supermarket, but if you have time the best version is home-made.

---

300 g (10½ oz) minced (ground) lamb

300 g (10½ oz) minced (ground) beef

300 g (10¼ oz) minced (ground) pork

½ teaspoon bicarbonate of soda (baking soda) dissolved in 2 teaspoons hot water

1 tablespoon finely chopped garlic

3 teaspoons sweet paprika

2 tablespoons finely chopped flat-leaf (Italian) parsley

1 teaspoon salt

freshly ground black pepper

olive oil, for frying

COMBINE all of the meats in a bowl with the bicarbonate of soda paste. Add all of the other ingredients for the cevaps and use your hands to squish the mixture together.

ROLL the mixture into balls slightly larger than a golf ball, then into 8–10 cm (3¼–4 inch) long cigars. Rest in the fridge for at least half an hour.

FRY in a hot frying pan with olive oil, browning for 3 minutes on each side, or until cooked through.

SERVE with ajvar relish (see recipe below) and a simple rocket (arugula) salad, rolled up in flatbread.

AJVAR RELISH

6 large red capsicums (peppers)

1 eggplant (aubergine)

2 large garlic cloves

3 tablespoons sunflower oil

1 teaspoon hot smoked paprika

a dash of apple cider vinegar or lemon juice

2 teaspoons salt

freshly ground black pepper

a pinch of sugar (optional)

AJVAR RELISH

PREHEAT the oven to 220°C (425°F). Roast the whole capsicums for 30 minutes, or until their skins blacken and blister, and they are soft. Cover with plastic wrap until cool then remove their skin and seeds. Reserve any juices.

COOK the eggplant on the stovetop directly over a high flame or on a barbecue grill until the skin blackens all over, turning every 5 minutes for even cooking. This will take about 20 minutes but will impart a beautiful smoky flavour.

BAKE the eggplant for 15 minutes, or until cooked through and soft. Halve lengthways, scoop out the flesh and discard the skin.

PULSE the capsicum, eggplant and garlic in a food processor until roughly chopped. Add the sunflower oil, paprika, vinegar, salt and pepper. Pulse until well combined.

TRANSFER the mixture to a medium saucepan. Add a few spoons of the reserved capsicum juice and a dash more vinegar.

GENTLY bring to the boil then reduce the heat and simmer for 20 minutes, stirring occasionally. Taste for seasoning and balance of flavours. Add a pinch of sugar if it's a little bitter.

COOL and store in a jar in the fridge. The relish tastes best the next day. It will keep for 2–3 weeks in the fridge.

Persian spiced lamb racks

• SERVES 4 •

There are so many ways to cook lamb and this is one of my favourites: the aromatic spices work beautifully with this sweet meat.

2 racks of lamb (about 6–7 cutlets each), French trimmed

olive oil, for rubbing

MARINADE

½ teaspoon ground cardamom

½ teaspoon ground cloves

½ teaspoon ground cinnamon

2 teaspoons ground cumin

2 teaspoons ground coriander

2 teaspoons crushed garlic

sea salt and freshly ground black pepper

juice of ½ lime

a dash of olive oil (about 2 teaspoons)

PREHEAT the oven to 200°C (400°F).

MIX all of the marinade ingredients together until it resembles a paste.

RUB the lamb with olive oil, salt and pepper.

SEAL the lamb by searing in a hot frying pan for a few minutes each side to brown.

SPREAD the marinade paste over the top side of the lamb racks and roast them on a baking tray for about 20 minutes for medium–rare or a little longer if you like it cooked more.

REMOVE the lamb from the oven and rest for 5 minutes covered in foil, then slice and serve.

DELICIOUS with honey baked carrots with caraway seeds (see page 96), quinoa detox salad (see page 74) or Persian rice and lentil bake (see page 88).

NOTE: French-trimmed lamb is well trimmed of excess fat and the bones are all scraped back so they look clean and pretty. If you are nice to your butcher, he will happily do this for you.

Tomato & pork cheek pasta

• SERVES 4 •

I recently discovered guanciale (cured pork cheek) at my Italian butcher's. It's fairly inexpensive and has a wonderful porky flavour, giving this fresh-tasting herb and tomato sauce great depth. You can use a mild pancetta for a similar result. This dish takes half an hour to prepare, but the time saver is that once it's gently cooking in the oven, your dinner duties are pretty much done.

450 g (1 lb) guanciale (cured pork cheek) or mild pancetta, rind removed and diced into 1 cm ($\frac{3}{8}$ inch) pieces

2 brown onions, finely diced

6 garlic cloves, finely chopped

1 x 800 g (1 lb 12 oz) tin crushed tomatoes

680 g (1 lb 8 oz) tomato passata (puréed tomatoes)

6 thyme sprigs

6 sage leaves

1 tablespoon chopped rosemary

1 teaspoon dried Greek oregano

2 fresh bay leaves

375 g (13 oz) farfalle pasta, cooked according to packet directions

parmesan cheese, to serve

PREHEAT the oven to 140°C (275°F).

FRY the diced guanciale over low heat in a flameproof casserole dish for about 10 minutes, or until lightly golden and the fat is translucent. Remove the meat from the dish and set aside.

FRY the onion in the pork fat over low heat until soft and golden.

RETURN the pork to the dish, add the garlic and sauté for 2 minutes.

STIR in the crushed tomatoes, passata and 125 ml (4 fl oz/$\frac{1}{2}$ cup) of water. Add the herbs and season with some freshly ground black pepper.

COVER the dish with baking paper and a tight-fitting lid. Bake in the oven for 1$\frac{1}{2}$ hours.

SEASON with salt and pepper and pour the sauce over the cooked pasta.

SERVE with shavings of parmesan.

NOTE: If the pork comes with rind, remove it in one piece and add it to the sauce before it goes into the oven. It will give the dish more flavour while it's cooking, but remember to remove and discard the rind before you serve up.

Miso salmon & soba noodles

• SERVES 4 •

This is a quickie but a goodie and it's my favourite midweek couch bowl meal. Rubbing the salmon fillets in miso and soy before cooking the fish gives it great flavour and a gorgeous caramelisation on the outside.

1½ teaspoons salt-reduced soy sauce

3 teaspoons miso paste

4 skinless salmon fillets, about
    180 g (6¼ oz) each

peanut oil, for frying

270 g (9½ oz) buckwheat (soba) noodles

1.25 kg (2 lb 12 oz) bok choy (pak choy),
    base removed, broken into
    individual leaves

DRESSING

3 tablespoons salt-reduced soy sauce

3 tablespoons peanut oil

2 tablespoons mirin (rice wine)

1 tablespoon rice vinegar

1 teaspoon honey

1 teaspoon chopped pickled ginger

HEAT a large saucepan of water and bring it to the boil.

COMBINE the soy sauce and miso paste and rub the mixture all over the salmon fillets.

MIX all of the dressing ingredients together in a jar, seal with a lid and shake.

COOK the salmon to medium–rare in a hot frying pan with a dash of peanut oil for about 3–4 minutes each side, depending on the thickness of the salmon, until the salmon is opaque. Remove from the heat.

MEANWHILE, cook the noodles in boiling water for about 4 minutes or according to the packet directions. Set a colander over the top of the saucepan and steam the bok choy, covered, at the same time.

DIVIDE the noodles among four bowls, top with the bok choy and the salmon and dress generously. Sometimes I scatter roasted sesame seeds on top.

Chilli basil chicken rice

· SERVES 4 ·

This is my go-to meal when I'm short on time and craving something clean and tasty. I often use chicken straight from the freezer: it's easier to slice wafer thin when frozen and thaws out in just minutes once sliced. This makes it a great last-minute dinner recipe. I always use free-range organic chicken when I can get it as I don't need any more hormones floating around my body!

80 ml (2½ fl oz/⅓ cup) peanut, coconut or grapeseed oil

300 g (10½ oz/1½ cups) jasmine or basmati rice

750 ml (26 fl oz/3 cups) boiling water

2 tablespoons finely chopped garlic

1 tablespoon finely chopped ginger

2 long red chillies, finely chopped

600 g (1 lb 5 oz) skinless chicken breast or thigh fillets, thinly sliced

4 spring onions (scallions), cut into 3 cm (1¼ inch) pieces

200 g (7 oz/4 cups firmly packed) basil leaves

2 tablespoons fish sauce

2 tablespoons salt-reduced soy sauce

1 lime, cut into wedges

25 g (1 oz/¼ cup) crispy fried shallots

1 small bunch of coriander (cilantro) leaves (optional)

HEAT 1 tablespoon of the peanut oil in a medium saucepan over medium–high heat and sauté the rice for 2 minutes, stirring continuously, to cook off the starch.

ADD the boiling water to the rice. Stir and cover with a lid.

REDUCE the heat to very low and simmer for 15 minutes without stirring. Turn off the heat and leave, covered, for a further 5 minutes before using.

HEAT the remaining oil in a wok or deep frying pan. Add the garlic, ginger and chilli and fry for about 1 minute, stirring occasionally for even cooking.

ADD the chicken and stir-fry for 5 minutes over high heat until the chicken turns white.

ADD the spring onions and basil leaves and fry for a further 3–5 minutes until the chicken is cooked through.

ADD the fish sauce and soy sauce and toss in the cooked rice.

TASTE for seasoning and add more fish sauce or soy sauce to adjust the saltiness.

SERVE in bowls with lime wedges, accompanied by the crispy fried shallots and sprigs of coriander (if using).

One-pot MEALS

There is a world of reasons to be time-poor and these reasons are multiplying exponentially with every time-saving gadget. Perhaps one of the reasons we are time-poor is that we stay up too late, because it's the only time of day something is not screaming, beeping or flashing at us. If you are a late-night TV watcher, you will be full-bottle on my favourite genre: the all-in-one tool ads. If you watch the right channels late at night, you will be familiar with an assortment of such wonders: there are garden power tools with interchangeable heads and there are kitchen tools with superpowers. But I still think the most valued tool in my kitchen is my large heavy-based pot. This chapter is full of my simple all-in-one-pot recipes, and I can assure you they are very popular with the dishwashing members of my family.

Beef rendang *with* coconut & cucumber salsa

• SERVES 4 •

This succulent aromatic curry wins hearts every time. Here's a time-saver: when collecting the ingredients for the spice paste, make up to four times the quantity and freeze it in portions.

---

1 kg (2 lb 4 oz) chuck steak, cut into 4 cm (1½ inch) cubes

2 tablespoons peanut or grapeseed oil

150 g (5½ oz) red Asian shallots, peeled and chopped

1 x 270 ml (9½ fl oz) tin coconut milk

3 kaffir lime (makrut) leaves

1 cinnamon stick

2 star anise

1 teaspoon kecap manis or tamarind paste

sugar (optional)

SPICE PASTE

1 teaspoon shrimp paste

2 lemongrass stems, tough outer leaves removed, roughly chopped

3 tablespoons finely chopped galangal (fresh or frozen)

3 tablespoons finely chopped fresh ginger

3 large garlic cloves

2–3 dried long red chillies

½ teaspoon turmeric

1½ tablespoons Malaysian curry powder

3 tablespoons peanut or grapeseed oil

PREHEAT the oven to 170°C (325°F).

MAKE the spice paste by putting all of the ingredients into a food processor and blitzing until smooth.

COMBINE the beef with the spice mixture in a large bowl and set aside.

HEAT the peanut oil in a large heavy-based flameproof casserole dish and lightly fry the shallots.

ADD the beef mixture and fry until lightly browned. You may need to do this in two batches, depending on the size of the dish.

ADD the coconut milk, kaffir lime leaves, cinnamon and star anise.

COVER with the lid and transfer to the oven to bake for 1½ hours, or until the beef is tender.

REMOVE from the oven and season with kecap manis, sugar, if needed, and salt to taste.

SERVE on rice, with the coconut and cucumber salsa (see recipe below), if desired.

NOTE: This curry freezes well and often comes on family holidays with us.

COCONUT & CUCUMBER SALSA

35 g (1¼ oz/½ cup) shredded coconut

½ telegraph (long) cucumber

¼ red onion

3 tablespoons lime juice

½ teaspoon sugar

pinch salt

COCONUT & CUCUMBER SALSA

PREHEAT the oven to 180°C (350°F).

SCATTER the coconut on a baking tray and lightly roast for 5–7 minutes until slightly golden. Allow to cool.

CHOP the cucumber and onion finely.

COMBINE all of the ingredients and serve as a side dish with the rendang.

Chicken Provençale

· SERVES 4 ·

Chicken is a favourite in our family, and this rustic French classic is full of simple ingredients with robust flavours. By the time it's baked you will be fully seduced by its wonderful aroma.

---

1 tablespoon butter

2 tablespoons olive oil

800 g (1 lb 12 oz) skinless chicken thigh fillets, halved

1 small onion, finely chopped

3 garlic cloves, thinly sliced

125 ml (4 fl oz/½ cup) white wine

1 tablespoon tomato paste (concentrated purée)

125 ml (4 fl oz/½ cup) chicken stock

75 g (2¾ oz/½ cup) pitted kalamata olives

2 tablespoons baby capers, drained and rinsed

2 fresh or dried bay leaves

a few thyme sprigs

4 sage leaves

a few oregano sprigs

1 yellow capsicum (pepper), cut into 1 cm (⅜ inch) squares

400 g (14 oz) medley cherry tomatoes, halved

PREHEAT the oven to 200°C (400°F).

MELT the butter and olive oil in a 30 cm (12 inch) diameter deep-sided ovenproof sauté pan.

ADD the chicken pieces and fry for a few minutes on each side until lightly browned. Add the onion and garlic and fry for a further 5 minutes, or until the onion has softened.

DEGLAZE the pan with the white wine and add the tomato paste. Increase the heat and cook for 5 minutes.

STIR in the stock, olives, capers and bay leaves. Scatter the herbs, capsicum and tomatoes over the top. Season with salt and pepper.

BAKE, covered with baking paper and the lid, for 30 minutes.

DELICIOUS served with baby smashed potatoes or rice.

Sausage & lentil casserole

• SERVES 4–6 •

For me there's something comforting about a sausage casserole, perhaps because it was my mum's Friday-night special. Everything went into the pot, to be served on toast within the hour. I've given this dish a lot of love over the years with the addition of creamy leeks, red wine and lentils instead of baked beans. Just like a pair of tracky dacks (sweatpants), it's become a winter favourite ... unlikely to win marks for presentation, but it sure will make you feel good.

olive oil, for frying and brushing

8–10 good-quality Italian sausages

3 leeks, white part only, sliced into 2 cm ($\frac{3}{4}$ inch) pieces

6 small pickling onions or whole French shallots

8–10 garlic cloves

210 g ($7\frac{1}{2}$ oz/1 cup) puy lentils, rinsed and drained

1 large carrot, halved lengthways and cut into 2 cm ($\frac{3}{4}$ inch) pieces

3 ripe tomatoes, approximately 350 g (12 oz), roughly chopped

20 g ($\frac{3}{4}$ oz/1 small bunch) thyme

2 bay leaves

500 ml (17 fl oz/2 cups) chicken stock

250 ml (9 fl oz/1 cup) red wine

6 thick slices sourdough bread

PREHEAT the oven to 200°C (400°F).

HEAT a dash of olive oil in a heavy-based ovenproof frying pan or flameproof casserole dish and lightly brown the sausages all over for a few minutes. Remove from the pan and set the sausages aside on a plate.

ADD the leek, onion and garlic to the same pan and gently fry over medium–low heat for 5–10 minutes until lightly golden. Stir occasionally for even cooking.

RETURN the sausages to the pan and add the remaining ingredients, except the bread, with 250 ml (9 fl oz/1 cup) of water.

COVER with a lid and bake for 45 minutes, or until the lentils are soft.

LIGHTLY brush the bread with olive oil and cook under the grill (broiler) on both sides before serving.

Chicken, black bean & corn hotpot

· SERVES 4–6 ·

Don't be overwhelmed by the list of ingredients. The many spices give this dish its great flavour.

1 large red onion, chopped

3 garlic cloves

olive oil, for frying

1 kg (2 lb 4 oz) skinless chicken thigh
fillets cut into 5 cm (2 inch) cubes

2 teaspoons dried oregano

2 teaspoons smoked paprika

1 teaspoon fennel seeds

3 teaspoons ground cumin

2 teaspoons ground coriander

1 cinnamon stick

1 teaspoon dried chilli flakes

250 ml (9 fl oz/1 cup) chicken stock

1 large red capsicum (pepper), seeded
and chopped into 2 cm ($\frac{3}{4}$ inch) pieces

200 g (7 oz/1 cup) corn kernels
(fresh off the cob)

4 large tomatoes, roughly chopped

1 x 400 g (14 oz) tin chopped tomatoes

2 x 400 g (14 oz) tins black beans,
drained and rinsed

1 handful of coriander (cilantro) leaves
and stems, washed

PREHEAT the oven to 180°C (350°F).

FRY the onion and garlic in a little olive oil in a heavy-based flameproof casserole dish until soft.

ADD the chicken and fry until lightly browned, then add all of the spices and fry for a few more minutes to coat the chicken.

ADD the chicken stock and stir for a minute. Add the capsicum, corn, fresh tomatoes and tinned tomatoes.

BAKE with the lid on for 45 minutes, adding the black beans for the last 15 minutes of cooking.

SERVE with fresh coriander.

DELICIOUS on brown rice, polenta, quinoa or couscous.

Chipotle turkey legs

Around Christmas and Thanksgiving, whether you celebrate these occasions or not, there is a lot of turkey going around. I have noticed that there is also a big supply of leftover gorgeous plump turkey legs that go cheap. These are absolutely delicious when slow-cooked, spiced up and then pulled.

1 tablespoon cumin seeds

1 tablespoon coriander seeds

1 teaspoon hot smoked paprika

1 teaspoon ground cinnamon

4 garlic cloves, finely chopped

120 g ($4\frac{1}{4}$ oz) chipotle chillies in adobo sauce (approximately 4 chillies and a bit of sauce)

2 tablespoons olive oil

2 big turkey legs, rinsed in cold water and patted dry with paper towel

1 large brown onion, finely diced

500 ml (17 fl oz/2 cups) chicken stock

6 ripe tomatoes, roughly chopped

1 handful of fresh coriander (cilantro) leaves and stems

PREHEAT the oven to 180°C (350°F).

BLITZ all of the spices, garlic, chipotle chillies and sauce together in a food processor until they form a paste.

HEAT the olive oil in a large heavy-based flameproof casserole dish. Lightly brown the turkey legs all over. Remove from the dish and put aside.

FRY the onion over low heat in the same dish for 5 minutes, or until soft. Add the spice paste and fry for a further 3 minutes over low heat.

RETURN the turkey legs to the dish and toss to coat in the spice paste. Add the stock and chopped tomatoes, and season with salt and pepper. Cover with baking paper and the lid.

BAKE for $2\frac{1}{2}$ hours, or until the meat is falling off the bones. Allow to cool slightly.

PULL the meat off the bones with a fork and return the meat to the sauce. Discard any sinew and bone.

REHEAT on the stovetop.

SERVE scattered with freshly chopped coriander, accompanied by rice, polenta or couscous.

NOTE: You can buy small tins of chipotle chillies in adobo sauce in international food stores or in the Mexican food section at good supermarkets.

One-pot spiced chicken *with* preserved lemon & green olives

· SERVES 4 ·

I know that for some people cooking is a chore, so I have included this fuss-free quick and delicious chicken one-pot wonder, which really does use just one pot and will always impress.

---

80 ml (2½ fl oz/⅓ cup) olive oil

1 large chicken, cut into quarters

2 red onions, quartered

4 potatoes, quartered

2 teaspoons ground cumin

2 teaspoons fennel seeds

1 teaspoon ground turmeric

2 teaspoons ground coriander

a few thyme sprigs

3 fresh bay leaves

2 tablespoons finely chopped
  preserved lemon

175 g (6 oz/1 cup) green olives

3 coriander (cilantro) sprigs, leaves picked
  and roots finely chopped

125 ml (4 fl oz/½ cup) verjuice

PREHEAT the oven to 180°C (350°F).

DRIZZLE half the olive oil over the base of a large heavy-based cast-iron casserole dish. Put the chicken pieces, skin side down, in the dish and brown over medium heat until golden. Turn the chicken pieces over and remove the dish from the heat.

POKE the onion and potato around and underneath the chicken. Scatter over the spices, thyme, bay leaves, preserved lemon, olives and chopped coriander root. Drizzle with the remaining oil, the verjuice and 125 ml (4 fl oz/½ cup) of water.

COVER with baking paper and the lid and bake for 1 hour.

SERVE scattered with the coriander leaves.

Ursula's pork & chicken adobo

· SERVES 6–8 ·

In this wonderful Filipino recipe my friend Ursula uses pork cutlets, belly or shoulder. You've got to love a dish in which all the ingredients are plonked into the pot and an hour or so later are transformed into a delectable dinner. Any leftovers are treasured as they make beautiful refried crispy adobo the next day...

1 kg (2 lb 4 oz) pork cutlets

1 kg (2 lb 4 oz) chicken thighs

125 ml (4 fl oz/½ cup) rice vinegar

60 ml (2 fl oz/¼ cup) water

125 ml (4 fl oz/½ cup) salt-reduced soy sauce

60 ml (2 fl oz/¼ cup) olive oil

1 garlic bulb, cloves separated, peeled and bruised (slightly crushed) with the back of a spoon

1 tablespoon whole black peppercorns

10 dried bay leaves, crumbled

1 tablespoon brown sugar (optional)

PUT all of the ingredients in a 4-litre (140 fl oz/16 cup) capacity saucepan, then cover with a lid and bring to the boil.

STIR and reduce the heat to a slow simmer. Leave the lid slightly ajar.

SIMMER for 1–1½ hours, or until the meat is tender and pulls apart easily.

DELICIOUS served with rice or buckwheat (soba) noodles with steamed cabbage.

Crispy refried adobo

Refrying any leftover adobo transforms it into the most gorgeous crispy meat. When I serve it with eggs, for breakfast, my kids think it's the most delicious thing ever.

3 tablespoons olive oil

1 cup of leftover pork and chicken adobo, bones removed

1–2 tablespoons finely chopped garlic

HEAT the olive oil in a nonstick frying pan and fry the meat and garlic until crispy. Continue stirring and pulling the meat apart as it cooks.

YUMMY in a bun, awesome in a lettuce leaf, or eat it by the spoonful!

Vegetable tagine *with* chickpeas

• SERVES 4 OR MORE •

This is a wonderful aromatic vegetarian dish. The home-made spice paste gives it great depth and can also be used as a marinade for seafood. If you are a meat lover, it's an awesome marinade for chicken, beef or a whole leg of lamb.

500 g (1 lb 2 oz) sweet potatoes

250 g (9 oz) kipfler potatoes, peeled

3 baby eggplants (aubergines)

1 zucchini (courgette)

3 tablespoons olive oil

8 baby French shallots, peeled

1 brown onion, roughly chopped

1 small fennel bulb, cut into 6 wedges

1 red capsicum (pepper), seeded and
   cut into strips

500 ml (17 fl oz/2 cups) vegetable stock

1 cinnamon stick

2 fresh bay leaves

10 pitted prunes

5 roma (plum) tomatoes, halved

1 x 400 g (14 oz) tin chickpeas (garbanzo
   beans), rinsed and drained

SPICE PASTE

1 roasted red capsicum (pepper)

3 teaspoons coriander seeds

3 teaspoons cumin seeds

3 garlic cloves

1 long red chilli

5 whole cloves

1 teaspoon smoked paprika

50 g (1¾ oz/1 cup) roughly chopped
   coriander (cilantro), including roots

25 g (1 oz/¾ cup) chopped flat-leaf
   (Italian) parsley

10 mint leaves

2 tablespoons chopped preserved lemon

3 tablespoons olive oil

PREHEAT the oven to 170°C (325°F).

DICE the sweet potatoes and potatoes into 4 cm (1½ inch) pieces. Quarter the baby eggplants and cut the zucchini lengthways and then into thirds. Set aside with the rest of the prepped vegetables while you make the spice paste.

PEEL and seed the roasted capsicum. Lightly toast the coriander and cumin seeds in a frying pan. Grind the roasted seeds together with the cloves using a mortar and pestle. Blend all of the spice paste ingredients together in a food processor until smooth.

HEAT the olive oil in a large heavy-based flameproof casserole dish. Add the shallots, onion and a tablespoon of water. Cover with the lid and gently cook over low heat for 8–10 minutes until softened and slightly golden. Check and toss a few times for even cooking.

ADD all of the vegetables and the spice paste to the dish. Lightly fry for about 10 minutes, stirring to coat evenly.

POUR in the stock, then add the cinnamon stick, bay leaves and prunes. Top with the tomatoes (don't stir in the tomatoes, they cook best on top so the flavours can intensify).

COVER the dish with baking paper and the lid and bake for about 1 hour until the vegetables are just tender. (Cooking time will vary, depending on how chunky or small you chop the vegies).

ADD the chickpeas for the final 15 minutes of cooking time.

DELICIOUS served on warm couscous, quinoa or rice with a dollop of yoghurt.

NOTE: If you prefer, you can use the finely grated zest and juice of 1 lemon instead of the preserved lemon in the spice paste.

Weekend DINNERS

It's amazing how often people drop by my place around lunch or dinner time on the weekends. We even get the odd brazen breakfast ambush.

My husband, Luc, sees the worst in it and thinks there are meal stealers around every corner. He would like a gated residence so he can eat in peace. On the other hand, I think it's human nature and I love to feed people. Whether they are led to our doorstep by their sense of smell, or sheer opportunism, I choose to see the best in their arrival and honour them with a meal. Luc thinks I am training people the way we train dogs — a gastronomical Pavlovian response — so I can have company when I am ready for my evening wine or Champagne.

Slow-roasted ocean trout *with* orange, lime & chilli relish

• SERVES 6 •

This is a gorgeous way to cook a whole side of trout. Slow-roasting it with the skin on imparts a beautiful flavour and makes it extra succulent and juicy.

2 limes

1 large orange

80 ml (2½ fl oz/⅓ cup) olive oil

1 spring onion (scallion), finely chopped

1 tablespoon finely chopped red chilli

15 g (¼ oz/¼ cup) coarsely chopped coriander (cilantro) leaves

2 tablespoons rice vinegar

2 tablespoons finely chopped fresh dill

½ teaspoon salt

10 grindings of white pepper

1 kg (2 lb 4 oz) side fillet of trout, skin on and pinbones removed

START by making the orange, lime and chilli relish: grate the zest of the limes and orange finely, reserving the zest for the marinade.

REMOVE the remaining skin and white pith from the orange and limes and cut the fruit into segments. Put these into a bowl and squeeze the empty fruit skins over them to extract any remaining juice. Stir in 3 tablespoons of the olive oil, the spring onion, chilli, coriander and rice vinegar and season with salt and pepper. Cover and set aside until needed.

PREHEAT the oven to 120°C (235°F).

COMBINE the remaining olive oil, reserved lime and orange zest, dill, salt and white pepper in a bowl.

LAY the trout, skin side down, on a large baking tray lined with baking paper and spread the mixture over the fish.

REST at room temperature for 10 minutes.

BAKE the trout for 25–30 minutes until the flesh is just opaque in the centre. Remove from the oven and rest for 10 minutes, covered with foil. Keep in mind that the fish will continue to cook a little more while resting.

BREAK the trout into large pieces using your hands, discard the skin and place the trout on a platter with the relish on the side.

Rotto herring

· SERVES 4 ·

I grew up in the Western Australian port city of Fremantle. I have fond memories of jumping into an old aluminium dinghy with Dad and heading 12 miles offshore, to Rottnest Island (Rotto) to catch herring. The best fish you will ever eat are the ones you catch yourself. This recipe works well with most oily fish.

---

3 tablespoons olive oil, plus extra
   for drizzling
10 herring, scaled, cleaned and
   filleted (skin on)

WARM DRESSING
zest of 1 orange
3 tablespoons orange juice
3 tablespoons lemon juice
a dash of olive oil
1 long red chilli, thinly sliced
1 large garlic clove, finely chopped
1 teaspoon fennel seeds
3 sevillano (queen) green olives, pitted
   and roughly chopped
1 large handful of coriander (cilantro)
   leaves, finely chopped

MIX all of the dressing ingredients together in a bowl, taste for balance of flavours and season with salt and pepper.

HEAT the olive oil in a large frying pan. Lay the herring fillets, skin side down, in the pan and fry for a few minutes until they start to curl up and are almost cooked through.

TURN the herring over and immediately pour the dressing over the fish in the pan. Cook for a further minute, or until the fish flakes easily and is cooked through.

SERVE in the pan at the table with an extra drizzle of olive oil.

DELICIOUS with a simple green salad and some crusty bread.

NOTE: If you don't have a large enough frying pan, cook the fish in two batches. Fry the first batch, remove it from the pan and fry the second batch; then return the first batch to the pan with the second batch, pour the dressing over and cook for 1 minute, or until the fish flakes easily.

Herby mustard fillet of beef

· SERVES 6–8 ·

When I want to cook something quick and fancy for a dinner party, I often buy a whole fillet of beef. If you are unsure how to prepare the fillet, have your butcher trim it for you, removing the side strap and sinew, then fold the thinner tail end under and secure it with some kitchen string. This will give the fillet a consistent shape and ensure even, perfect cooking.

1.5 kg (3 lb 5 oz) fillet of beef, trimmed of fat and sinew

100 ml (3½ fl oz) olive oil

4 garlic cloves, finely chopped

1 tablespoon wholegrain mustard

2 tablespoons finely chopped rosemary

2 tablespoons finely chopped thyme

creamed horseradish and dijon mustard, for serving

PREHEAT the oven to 200°C (400°F).

RUB the beef fillet with 2 tablespoons of the olive oil and season with salt and pepper.

HEAT a large nonstick frying pan or barbecue hotplate and sear the beef for 8–10 minutes, turning regularly until browned all over. Transfer to a baking tray or roasting tin.

MIX the garlic, mustard and herbs with salt, pepper and the remaining olive oil in a bowl.

RUB the garlic mixture evenly over the beef.

BAKE for approximately 25 minutes for medium–rare. Test by cutting into the centre of the fillet with a knife: it should still be quite pink, but not raw. Take it out of the oven a little underdone, as it continues to cook while resting.

REST the beef in a warm place, covered with foil, for 8–10 minutes before slicing and serving.

SERVE with a dollop of creamed horseradish and mustard or delicious with a simple side, such as baked vegies with garlic (see page 93) or green beans, broccolini and pancetta (see page 76).

Slow-baked lamb shoulder

• SERVES 6 •

If you could rate a dish on smell alone, this little lamb shoulder would score a perfect ten! Not only does this dish cook itself, it warms up the house and is an alluring five-hour torment for my hungry husband.

½ preserved lemon, rind only

4 garlic cloves

1 teaspoon ground cinnamon

1 teaspoon ground cumin

1 teaspoon ground coriander

1 teaspoon fennel seeds

2 tablespoons olive oil

lamb shoulder joint with bone,
   approximately 2.25 kg (5 lb)

250 ml (9 fl oz/1 cup) white wine
   or verjuice

PREHEAT the oven to 160°C (315°F).

BLITZ the preserved lemon rind, garlic, spices and olive oil in a food processor until it forms a rough paste.

PLACE the lamb in a heavy-based casserole dish and rub the paste over the top and sides of the meat.

POUR the wine and 250 ml (9 fl oz/1 cup) of water over and cover with a sheet of baking paper and the lid to create a good seal.

BAKE for 5 hours (or 4 hours at 170°C/325°F). Remove from the oven when the meat is tender and easily falls off the bone, then rest for 10–15 minutes in the casserole dish, covered.

TRANSFER the lamb to a large serving platter and use two forks to shred the meat off the bone. Discard the bone and any fat, then skim the fat from the juices in the casserole dish. Carefully pour the juices all over the meat and serve. This dish goes beautifully with muhammara and tzatziki as accompaniments (see pages 164 and 172) and also the Persian rice and lentil bake (see page 88).

Flattened Greek spatchcocks

· SERVES 4 ·

These little spatchcocks, once marinated and cooked, are really yummy and crispy. You can replace the small birds with two whole medium-size chickens, and you will have enough to feed eight people.

4 x 400 g (14 oz) spatchcocks (poussins)

50 g (1¾ oz/1 cup) chopped coriander (cilantro) leaves

30 g (1 oz/1 cup) chopped flat-leaf (Italian) parsley

20 g (¾ oz/1 cup) mint leaves

8 garlic cloves

125 ml (4 fl oz/½ cup) lemon juice

125 ml (4 fl oz/½ cup) olive oil

1½ teaspoons sea salt

PREHEAT the oven to 180°C (350°F).

FLATTEN the spatchcocks: partially debone using poultry scissors or a sharp knife to cut down both sides of the backbone, from the cavity to the neck. Discard the bones or freeze them to make stock later. Remove the little rib bones at the top of the breast. Pierce the breastbone in the middle with a sharp knife and then press down on the bird using your hands to completely flatten.

RINSE each spatchcock under cold water, pat dry with paper towel and put them into a clean dish.

BLITZ all of the remaining ingredients in a food processor to a fine consistency.

POUR the blended marinade over the spatchcocks and coat generously to marinate for at least 3 hours. I usually do it overnight for best results.

SPREAD the spatchcocks on a baking tray and roast for 45 minutes, or until crispy on the outside and cooked through (if using chicken, roast for 1–1½ hours).

DELICIOUS with Greek goddess salad (see page 72) or kale, pine nuts, lemon and feta (see page 98).

Green pea, leek & feta tart

• SERVES 4–6 •

I love skipping steps when it doesn't compromise a good meal. There is no pre-baking of pastry if you bake this tart in the bottom of the oven like a pizza.

---

1 quantity savoury shortcrust pastry
(see recipe below)

1 leek, white part only, halved lengthways,
washed and thinly sliced

1 tablespoon butter

100 g ($3\frac{1}{2}$ oz) feta cheese

4 eggs

355 g ($12\frac{1}{2}$ oz/$2\frac{1}{2}$ cups) frozen peas,
thawed

310 ml ($10\frac{3}{4}$ fl oz/$1\frac{1}{4}$ cups) thin
(pouring) cream

PREHEAT the oven to 170°C (325°F).

LINE a lightly greased 25 cm (10 inch) diameter flan tin with 3 cm ($1\frac{1}{4}$ inch) sides with the thinly rolled shortcrust pastry. Trim the excess pastry from around the edge of the tin and put it in the fridge to chill for 20 minutes.

SAUTÉ the leek in the butter for 5–8 minutes until soft, then set aside to cool a little.

CRUMBLE the feta over the chilled pastry base and spread the cooled leek over evenly.

BLITZ the eggs, peas and cream in a food processor until smooth, then carefully pour into the pastry case.

BAKE for approximately 20 minutes on the bottom shelf of the oven (this will help to ensure a crispy base), then move the tart to the middle shelf and cook for a further 10 minutes. It will be ready when the mixture sets and the pastry has a golden tinge.

SAVOURY SHORTCRUST PASTRY

*Makes enough pastry for a 25–35 cm
(10–14 inch) tart*

125 g ($4\frac{1}{2}$ oz) butter

250 g (9 oz/$1\frac{2}{3}$ cups) plain (all-purpose)
flour

a pinch of salt

60 ml (2 fl oz/$\frac{1}{4}$ cup) iced water

SAVOURY SHORTCRUST PASTRY

PULSE the butter, flour and salt in a food processor until it resembles breadcrumbs.

ADD the iced water and pulse six more times to just combine.

TIP the pastry out onto a clean work surface and push it together with your hands, working the pastry until it comes together. Form into a ball, wrap in plastic wrap and chill in the fridge for 20 minutes before rolling.

ROLL the pastry out between two sheets of plastic wrap until you have a 35 cm (14 inch) circle about 3 mm ($\frac{1}{8}$ inch) thick.

Mexican beef pies

• MAKES 12 •

I love a good meat pie. It's my comfort food — a complete meal, all wrapped up in golden crispy pastry. If you have a crowd coming over on the weekend, bake the pies a few hours beforehand, then reheat when ready to serve. They are easier to handle when they have rested. If you eat them straight from the oven you may need a plate, knife and fork. Either way they are utterly delicious.

2 tablespoons olive oil

2 brown onions, finely chopped

2 garlic cloves, finely chopped

1.5 kg (3 lb 5 oz) chuck steak, cut into 2.5 cm (1 inch) cubes

2 teaspoons fennel seeds

3 teaspoons ground cumin

2 teaspoons ground coriander

2 teaspoons hot smoked paprika

1 teaspoon dried oregano

2 x 400 g (14 oz) tins chopped tomatoes

4 chipotle chillies in adobo sauce, finely chopped

2 x 400 g (14 oz) tins black beans, rinsed and drained

1 handful of coriander (cilantro) leaves

8 sheets ready-made puff pastry

200 g (7 oz/2 cups) grated cheddar cheese

2 egg yolks, whisked

PREHEAT the oven to 170°C (325°F).

HEAT the olive oil in a large heavy-based flameproof casserole dish and lightly fry the onions and garlic for 8–10 minutes until soft.

ADD the steak, spices and oregano, stir to coat, then gently brown for about 10 minutes, stirring occasionally so the spices don't stick and burn.

STIR in the tomatoes and chipotle chillies.

COVER with baking paper and the lid and bake for $1\frac{1}{2}$ hours, or until the meat is tender.

ADD the black beans for the last 15 minutes of cooking time, then add the coriander and season with salt and pepper when you remove it from the oven.

COOL the mixture before you make the pies.

PREHEAT the oven to 200°C (400°F) and line two large baking trays with baking paper.

ASSEMBLE the pies by cutting the puff pastry sheets into 13 cm (5 inch) rounds: you can get three rounds from each standard sheet if you cut out two on the diagonal and then join the excess pastry from the corners together, re-roll and cut out the third round.

PLACE a pastry round in a shallow 12 cm ($4\frac{1}{2}$ inch) diameter bowl, spoon in about half a cup of the mixture, top with a spoonful of grated cheddar cheese and cover with another pastry round. Pinch around the edges to seal them together, then carefully flip the pie upside down onto a clean surface and fold in the edges of the pastry.

BRUSH the top of each pie with the egg yolk and set them out on the prepared trays. Repeat until you have 12 pies.

BAKE for 25–30 minutes, or until golden and the bases are crisp.

Portuguese chicken wings

· SERVES 4–6 ·

This is a tasty, cheap way to feed your family or a crowd; the spectacular aroma on the barbecue draws everyone in. If you don't own any large metal skewers you can use bamboo skewers, just soak them in water for 30 minutes before use to prevent burning.

14–16 plump chicken wings

12 fresh bay leaves, whole

MARINADE

juice and zest of 1 lemon

3 large garlic cloves, finely chopped

1½ tablespoons smoked paprika

3 tablespoons olive oil

2 fresh bay leaves, finely chopped

1 teaspoon dried oregano

1 handful oregano leaves, finely chopped

1 teaspoon salt

COMBINE the marinade ingredients in a bowl.

CUT the tip off each chicken wing and discard (or freeze them to make stock later).

COAT the chicken wings in the marinade and place in the fridge for at least 1 hour.

SKEWER the wings and thread the bay leaves between the chicken pieces. Depending on the length of skewers, you might fit 3–4 wings on each.

COOK over a barbecue or in a chargrill pan over medium–low heat for 30–40 minutes, rotating for even cooking and basting with any remaining marinade.

SERVE with a gorgeous salad. See Salads to Share (page 66).

NOTE: If you have a lid on your barbecue, close it; keeping the heat in will speed up the cooking time.

Crispy skin barramundi *with* chilli lime tamarind sauce

Crunchy, succulent, sweet and salty: if this is what you feel like eating, this dish ticks all the boxes.

100 ml (3½ fl oz) peanut oil

1 tablespoon coriander roots, finely chopped (reserve leaves for garnish)

1 tablespoon finely chopped red Asian shallot

1 tablespoon finely chopped garlic

1 tablespoon finely chopped red chilli

2 teaspoons finely chopped fresh ginger

75 g (2¾ oz/½ cup) crumbled palm sugar (jaggery)

90 g (3¼ oz/⅓ cup) tamarind purée

1 tablespoon light soy sauce

2 teaspoons fish sauce

2 spring onions (scallions), cut into 2 cm (¾ inch) lengths

4 barramundi fillets (skin on), or other firm white-fleshed fish, about 180 g (6¼ oz) each

rice, to serve

PREHEAT the oven to 200°C (400°F).

HEAT 3 tablespoons of the peanut oil in a medium frying pan. Add the coriander root, shallot, garlic, chilli and ginger and gently fry for a few minutes until fragrant.

ADD 80 ml (2½ fl oz/⅓ cup) of water, the palm sugar, tamarind purée, soy sauce and fish sauce. Simmer and reduce for 2–3 minutes. Check the balance of sweet, sour and salty flavours. Adjust accordingly.

ADD the spring onions and cook in the reduced sauce for 2 minutes, or until just soft. Set aside until ready to serve.

HEAT the remaining peanut oil in a clean ovenproof frying pan over medium heat. Fry the fish, skin side down, for 6–7 minutes until crispy. Turn it over and fry for 2 more minutes.

TRANSFER the pan to the oven for 3–5 minutes, depending on the thickness of the fillets, until cooked through.

REHEAT the sauce just before serving.

SERVE the fish on a bed of cooked rice, spoon the sauce over, and garnish with fresh coriander sprigs.

DELICIOUS with steamed choy sum.

Party Tricks

I love a good party. I'm not sure why, really. It could be because I get the chance to sing and dance, or to see all of my friends at once. Perhaps it's because, as I'm the youngest in a big family, it feels a lot like home: cooking in the midst of chaos and spoiling everyone with food.

Parties provide me with a foodie focal point. I can make lots of food because there are plenty of mouths to feed and plenty of hands to do the dishes.

These party tricks have been successful at my own parties, and paid my mortgage while I was burning the candle at both ends as a caterer and single mum. I've shared them here because parties, like pregnancies, are not always planned and can sneak up on you before you are ready.

These recipes are the best of several worlds: quick, simple, fun *and* yummy, and great for feeding a crowd.

Mixed olives *with* orange, fennel & chilli

I think this little marinade for olives is the absolute best. Perhaps it's because it is a combination of all my favourite ingredients.

---

500 g (1 lb 2 oz) mixed olives in brine

zest of 1 small orange, **in thin strips**

1 teaspoon fennel seeds

1 small red chilli, **seeded and thinly sliced**

1 garlic clove, finely chopped

2 tablespoons olive oil

1 small handful of coriander (cilantro) leaves (if serving right away)

COMBINE all of the ingredients in a bowl and marinate for at least 2 hours for the flavours to develop.

STORE in the fridge. This will keep for a few weeks if you add the fresh coriander before serving.

Oysters *with* chilli, tomato, lime salsa

• MAKES 2 CUPS OF SALSA FOR 4 DOZEN OYSTERS •

When I have promised to 'bring a plate' but run out of time, I thank King Neptune for creating one of our ocean's tastiest little morsels: the oyster. Fabulous au naturel or jazzed up with a little bowl of salsa on the side. The trick to making a good salsa is ensuring all your ingredients are finely diced.

---

80 ml ($2\frac{1}{2}$ fl oz/$\frac{1}{3}$ cup) lime juice

2 tablespoons olive oil

1 teaspoon salt

1 teaspoon sugar

1 long red chilli, seeded and finely chopped

$\frac{1}{2}$ red onion, finely diced

2 large tomatoes, seeded and finely chopped

2 garlic cloves, finely chopped

20 g ($\frac{3}{4}$ oz/$\frac{1}{3}$ cup) finely chopped coriander (cilantro) leaves

crushed ice, to serve

4 dozen oysters, shucked

COMBINE the lime juice, olive oil, salt and sugar in a bowl.

STIR in the finely chopped chilli, onion, tomato, garlic and coriander.

TASTE for a good balance of seasoning and adjust according to taste. Transfer to a serving bowl.

SET the bowl of salsa in the centre of a large platter, scatter crushed ice evenly around the bowl and arrange the oysters on top of the ice for guests to help themselves.

Hummus

Everyone loves hummus in our household! It's so much tastier (not to mention cheaper) when you make a fresh batch at home. I like to make mine extra creamy by slowly drizzling in the lemon juice, tahini and olive oil. Sometimes I zap it in the microwave as it is delicious served warm with a drizzle of extra virgin olive oil and grilled Turkish bread. Any leftovers make a tasty addition to lunch rolls and wraps, and for a fun variation you can add steamed soft beetroot (beets) to make it bright purple.

---

250 g (9 oz/1$\frac{1}{4}$ cups) dried chickpeas

2 dried bay leaves

3–4 garlic cloves, crushed

1$\frac{1}{2}$ teaspoons sea salt

2 teaspoons cumin seeds, lightly roasted and ground

80 ml (2$\frac{1}{2}$ fl oz/$\frac{1}{3}$ cup) lemon juice, or more to taste

3 tablespoons tahini

3–4 tablespoons olive oil

smoked paprika and extra virgin olive oil, to serve

SOAK the chickpeas in 1 litre (35 fl oz/4 cups) of water overnight, or for at least 6 hours.

DRAIN the soaked chickpeas. Put them in a saucepan with 2 litres (70 fl oz/8 cups) of fresh cold water and the bay leaves. Bring to the boil. Reduce the heat to low and simmer for 45–60 minutes until soft and tender.

DRAIN the cooked chickpeas in a colander, reserving 250 ml (9 fl oz/1 cup) of the cooking liquid. Discard the bay leaves.

BLEND the chickpeas in a food processor or upright blender with the garlic, salt, cumin seeds and half of the reserved liquid until smooth. (Add more liquid if needed.)

ADD the lemon juice, tahini and olive oil slowly while the food processor is still running; this will make it super-creamy. Taste for the balance of flavours and seasoning.

SERVE in a bowl, sprinkled with paprika and drizzled with extra virgin olive oil.

DELICIOUS with grilled Turkish bread.

Jerusalem artichoke filo tartlets

• MAKES 48 •

These delicious miniature tarts are the first thing to be devoured at any party. Crispy, creamy and fresh ... all in one mouthful!

---

300 g (10½ oz) Jerusalem artichokes, approximately 200 g (7 oz) when peeled

1 lemon, for squeezing

250 ml (9 fl oz/1 cup) milk

185 ml (6 fl oz/¾ cup) thickened (whipping) cream

2 large eggs

25 g (1 oz/¼ cup) grated parmesan cheese

7½ sheets ready-made filo pastry

120 g (4¼ oz) butter, melted

PEEL the Jerusalem artichokes with a potato peeler and put them straight into water with a squeeze of lemon to stop them discolouring. Drain and weigh to check the peeled weight.

CUT the artichokes into 2 cm (¾ inch) pieces and put them into a saucepan with the milk and 500 ml (17 fl oz/2 cups) of water. Bring to the boil, then reduce the heat to simmer for 25–30 minutes until the artichokes are tender. Drain in a colander for 10 minutes and allow to cool slightly.

BLITZ the artichokes in a food processor with the cream, eggs, parmesan and salt and pepper until smooth. Set aside.

PREHEAT the oven to 180°C (350°F).

ASSEMBLE the tarts: stick 3 sheets of filo pastry together by brushing melted butter between each sheet and then on top. Cut the layered pastry sheets into 40 mini 5.5 cm (2¼ inch) squares. Lay 2 squares together on the diagonal to form a star shape and press buttered-side down into a 24-hole mini muffin tin. Continue until you have made 20 tart cases. Repeat the process with 3 more sheets of filo pastry for another 20 tart cases and then with the remaining 1½ sheets (cut the whole sheet in half to make 3 half-size sheets) and assemble in the same way to make 8 more tart cases. Discard any leftover pastry.

FILL the pastry cases with one heaped teaspoon of artichoke mixture, being careful not to overfill with mixture as it will stick to the tin.

BAKE for 15–20 minutes, until the tarts puff up and the pastry is golden and crisp.

SERVE warm as is, or with dollops of green olive tapenade (see page 168).

NOTE: If you are feeling fancy, you can fry a heaped tablespoon of capers in 125 ml (4 fl oz/½ cup) of olive oil to make them crispy, drain on paper towel and scatter them over the tarts.

Muhammara (red pepper dip)

• MAKES ABOUT 440 G (15½ OZ/2 CUPS) •

Muhammara is a stunning red pepper dip and condiment made in Middle Eastern countries such as Lebanon and Syria. The combination of the smoky roasted red peppers with the tangy pomegranate syrup and earthy walnuts brings a magical blend of flavours and textures to the table. The first time I tasted muhammara was at David Coomer's tapas restaurant in Perth and I had to go home and recreate it based on that delicious experience.

---

4 large red capsicums (peppers), approximately 900 g (2 lb)

3 garlic cloves, chopped

1½ teaspoons smoked paprika

2 teaspoons cumin seeds, toasted and ground

1 teaspoon chilli flakes

3 tablespoons lemon juice

115 g (4 oz/1 cup) raw walnuts, lightly roasted

3 tablespoons olive oil, plus extra to serve

2 tablespoons pomegranate molasses

95 g (3¼ oz/⅓ cup) plain yoghurt

1 small handful of mint leaves

pomegranate seeds, to scatter (optional)

PREHEAT the oven to 180°C (350°F).

GRILL the capsicums over a stovetop gas burner or barbecue for 10 minutes, rotating occasionally to slightly blacken their skins all over. This will impart a wonderful smoky flavour.

TRANSFER to the oven for a further 15–20 minutes until roasted and soft.

COVER the roasted capsicums with plastic wrap in a bowl to sweat and cool.

PEEL the capsicums and discard their peel, stem and seeds.

BLEND the capsicum flesh in a food processor with the garlic, paprika, cumin seeds, chilli and lemon juice until smooth.

ADD the walnuts (reserving a tablespoon for garnish) and then pulse three or four times to just break them up, as you want a grainy texture.

TRANSFER the mixture to a bowl and fold in the olive oil and pomegranate molasses, then season with salt and pepper. If you want more tang, add more pomegranate molasses.

SERVE spooned out on a plate drizzled with yoghurt and olive oil and topped with mint leaves, pomegranate seeds (if using), and the reserved walnuts, lightly broken.

DELICIOUS as a dip with grilled Turkish bread, but also a great condiment for meats. It's particularly yummy with my slow-baked lamb shoulder (see page 144).

Ceviche in a silver spoon

• MAKES ABOUT 20 •

This little spoonful of South American-style marinated fish will win hearts with its fresh, bright zingy flavours. The best thing about ceviche is that there is no heat required as the fish 'cooks' in the citrus juice, giving it a wonderful texture. With this in mind, make sure you source very fresh fish (most white-fleshed fish are suitable).

---

2 teaspoons sugar

1 teaspoon salt

200 g (7 oz) skinless snapper fillet, pinbones removed

125 ml (4 fl oz/$\frac{1}{2}$ cup) lime juice

1 long red chilli, finely chopped

1 garlic clove, crushed

1 teaspoon finely grated fresh ginger

$\frac{1}{2}$ small red onion, finely chopped

1 large tomato, seeded and finely chopped

3 heaped tablespoons finely chopped coriander (cilantro) leaves

a dash of olive oil

CUT the fish into 1 cm ($\frac{3}{8}$ inch) cubes and transfer to a bowl.

SPRINKLE the sugar and salt evenly over the fish, then pour the lime juice all over.

ADD the chilli, garlic and ginger and allow to marinate in the fridge for 10 minutes or a little longer, depending on how well 'cooked' through you like it.

ADD the onion, tomato, coriander and olive oil.

STIR and taste for a nice balance of sweet, salty and sour flavours. Adjust to suit your tastebuds.

SERVE in spoons and eat immediately.

Green olive tapenade

This is a gorgeous dip for a party, and also great dolloped on top of my Jerusalem artichoke filo tartlets (see page 163). Any left over tapenade is delicious in sandwiches or served with grilled chicken and fish.

90 g (3¼ oz/½ cup) pitted green olives

1 large garlic clove, finely chopped

1 spring onion (scallion), finely chopped

15 g (½ oz/½ cup) roughly chopped
   flat-leaf (Italian) parsley

75 g (2¾ oz/½ cup) shelled pistachio nuts

2 tablespoons grated parmesan cheese

2 tablespoons olive oil

2 tablespoons lemon juice

1 teaspoon grated lemon zest

freshly ground black pepper

a pinch of salt

PULSE all of the ingredients together in a food processor until combined, but still with a slightly chunky texture.
SERVE with crackers.

Fig & prosciutto sushi

This dish requires no cooking so it's a perfect summertime party trick. When purchasing figs, go for the plump round variety as they will give you a better shape. If you can only find the long pear-shaped figs, just trim a little off the top end ... and eat it: cook's privilege!

4 plump fresh figs

160–180 g (5¾–6¼ oz) Danish or
   marinated feta cheese

8 thin slices of prosciutto, rind
   removed

16 basil leaves

CUT each fig in half from top to bottom.
CUT or break the feta into 8 portions of about 20 g (¾ oz) each and use your fingers to shape them into rounds about 3 cm (1¼ inches) diameter and 5 mm (¼ inch) thick.
LAY the prosciutto out on a board or clean work surface.
LAYER a basil leaf, a round of feta and another basil leaf on the cut side of a fig half, then roll in a strip of prosciutto. Set aside on a dish lined with slightly damp paper towel.
REPEAT until you have 8 rolled pieces. Cover and refrigerate for at least 30 minutes before cutting.
SERVE by cutting each piece in half at the equator and present with the fig face up on a platter.

Chicken & pistachio sangas

• MAKES 9 SANDWICHES (27 FINGER SERVINGS) •

The only time I buy a soft commercial loaf of bread is when I am making these sandwiches. The loaves usually have 18 perfect slices, excluding the crusts.

---

900 g (2 lb) boneless skinless
   chicken thighs

1 teaspoon finely chopped garlic

3 tablespoons olive oil

a squeeze of lemon juice

a pinch of salt

freshly ground black pepper

1 loaf sliced white and/or multigrain
   bread

MAYO MIX

85 g (3 oz/$\frac{1}{3}$ cup) mayonnaise

70 g (2$\frac{1}{2}$ oz/$\frac{1}{4}$ cup) plain yoghurt

65 g (2$\frac{1}{2}$ oz/$\frac{1}{4}$ cup) sour cream

15 g ($\frac{1}{2}$ oz/$\frac{1}{4}$ cup) chopped chives

20 g ($\frac{3}{4}$ oz/$\frac{1}{3}$ cup) chopped coriander
   (cilantro) leaves

40 g (1$\frac{1}{2}$ oz/$\frac{1}{3}$ cup) roughly chopped
   pistachio nuts

2 tablespoons chopped flat-leaf
   (Italian) parsley

finely grated zest of 1 lemon

PREHEAT the oven to 180°C (350°F). Line a baking tray with baking paper.

TRIM the excess fat from the chicken thighs.

MIX together the garlic, olive oil, lemon juice, salt and pepper in a bowl and toss with the chicken.

BAKE the chicken thighs on the prepared tray, covered with foil, for 30 minutes, or until cooked through. The cooking time will depend on the size of the thighs.

REMOVE the cooked chicken from the oven, allow to cool and then dice into small cubes.

COMBINE the mayo mix ingredients together in a bowl. Mix in the diced chicken.

SET 9 slices of bread out on a clean surface and spoon a generous amount of the chicken and mayo mix evenly over each piece, then cover with another slice of bread. Place in stacks of 2 and cover immediately with a lightly dampened clean cloth to retain freshness.

REMOVE the crusts and cut each sandwich into 3 strips. I usually cut the stacks of 2 sandwiches together to keep the size consistent.

MAKE and cut the sandwiches a few hours before serving, then place on a platter, cover with damp paper towel and refrigerate. This will keep them super-fresh!

NOTE: Use an electric bread knife or good-quality bread knife when cutting for best results.

Cheeky Greek chicken rice balls
with tzatziki

• MAKES ABOUT 30 RICE BALLS • MAKES 400 G (14 OZ/2 CUPS) TZATZIKI •

This is one of those recipes I threw together when I was in a hurry and it turned out to be the party favourite. The cheeky addition of tinned dolmades gives it great texture and flavour.

---

2 tablespoons olive oil, plus extra for frying sample ball

1 brown onion, finely chopped

2 garlic cloves, finely chopped

2 teaspoons ground cumin

2 teaspoons ground coriander

1 teaspoon ground cinnamon

600 g (1 lb 5 oz) minced (ground) chicken

1 x 280 g (10 oz) tin dolmades (stuffed vine leaves), drained and finely chopped

finely grated zest of 1 lime

30 g (1 oz/¼ cup) pitted green olives, finely chopped

1 large handful of coriander (cilantro) leaves, finely chopped

1 egg

1 teaspoon salt

freshly ground black pepper

PREHEAT the oven to 180°C (350°F).

HEAT the olive oil in a small frying pan and fry the onion and garlic for 3 minutes, or until soft. Add the spices and fry for 1 minute. Transfer to a large bowl.

ADD the remaining ingredients to the bowl and mix with your hands until they are well combined.

ROLL one sample ball and fry in a lightly oiled pan until cooked. Taste for seasoning and adjust if necessary.

ROLL the mixture into golf-ball size balls, using damp hands, and set them out on a generously oiled nonstick baking tray.

BAKE for 25 minutes, or until cooked through and slightly golden on the outside. Turn over halfway through the cooking time.

SERVE with tzatziki (see recipe below).

TZATZIKI

juice of ½ lemon

2 garlic cloves, grated

1 teaspoon sugar

½ teaspoon salt

2 Lebanese (short) cucumbers, seeded and grated

260 g (9¼ oz/1 cup) Greek-style yoghurt

1 tablespoon finely chopped dill or mint

TZATZIKI

COMBINE the lemon juice, garlic, sugar and salt in a bowl.

STRAIN the cucumber through a sieve to squeeze out excess juice, then add it to the mixture in the bowl.

STIR in the yoghurt and dill and refrigerate until ready to serve.

Sweet and NICE

This is the chapter for those of you with willpower. Congratulations! You have arrived at the chapter written by the very skinny and (seldom seen) sensible me. Ha!

In writing these healthy dessert recipes I have tapped the old favourites on the shoulder so they can be rediscovered through a healthier lens. There is plenty of sugar in fruit and yoghurt is kinder to the waistline than cream. Jelly has been enchanting kids for generations and is still lots of fun without our overused friend, sugar. Even if you follow a sugar-, wheat- or dairy-free diet, there is no reason why you should go without dessert!

Mango & passionfruit mousse

• SERVES 6 •

This is a quick, light, summery dessert for a dinner party when mangoes are cheap and in season.

---

3 large ripe mangoes, peeled, stoned and diced

75 g (2¾ oz/⅓ cup) caster (superfine) sugar

1 tablespoon lime juice

3 teaspoons powdered gelatine

3 tablespoons boiling water

355 g (12½ oz/1⅓ cups) Greek-style yoghurt, plus extra, for serving

2 large egg whites

4 passionfruit

BLITZ 300 g (10½ oz) of the mango flesh with the sugar and lime juice in an upright blender for about 20 seconds until smooth. Reserve the remaining flesh.

WHISK the gelatine in a small bowl with the boiling water until it dissolves. Add to the mango mixture in the blender and blitz for a further 5 seconds.

COMBINE the yoghurt and blended mango mixture in a large bowl.

BEAT the egg whites to soft peaks in a clean glass or metal bowl, then gently fold into the yoghurt and mango mixture until smooth.

TOSS the remaining mango flesh and the passionfruit pulp in a small bowl and divide evenly among six glasses.

SPOON the mousse over the fruit, cover and refrigerate for 4 hours, or until set.

SERVE with an extra dollop of yoghurt.

NOTE: Coconut yoghurt also works well with this dessert.

Spiced sugarless stewed plums

· SERVES 4–6 ·

My mother-in-law, Sue, is so sweet she doesn't need sugar. She has been a wonderful help with this book and this recipe is especially for her.

---

grated zest of 1 orange

juice of 3 oranges

a pinch of ground cinnamon

a pinch of ground allspice

1 kg (2 lb 4 oz) plums, halved, stones removed

HEAT the orange zest and juice with the spices in a large frying pan and bring to the boil.

REDUCE the heat and add the plum halves, cut side down. Simmer for 3 minutes.

TURN the plums over and cook for a further 3 minutes.

TURN off the heat and allow the fruit to cool in the pan. The longer you leave it, the better the flavour.

OPTIONAL: Remove the skins once cooled, for an even more luscious result.

DELICIOUS served with cream or ice cream.

Mango, almond & coconut cake

• SERVES 8–10 •

This is a wonderfully moist gluten- and dairy-free cake. If it's not mango season you can use frozen mango cheeks instead. Make sure they are completely thawed and squeeze out any excess water before blitzing.

550 g (1 lb 4 oz) mango flesh
   (approximately 2–3 fresh mangoes)
8 eggs
180 g (6¼ oz) caster (superfine) sugar
½ teaspoon natural vanilla extract
300 g (10½ oz/3 cups) almond meal
65 g (2½ oz/1 cup) shredded coconut
2 teaspoons baking powder, sifted
a pinch of salt
coconut yoghurt, for serving

PREHEAT a fan-forced oven to 160°C (315°F) or a regular oven to 170°C (325°F). Grease and line a 23 cm (9 inch) round cake tin with baking paper.

BLITZ the mango, eggs, sugar and vanilla together in a food processor until smooth.

ADD the remaining ingredients, except the coconut yoghurt, and pulse gently to just combine.

POUR the mixture into the prepared cake tin.

BAKE for 55–65 minutes until golden and firm. Check whether the cake is cooked by inserting a skewer into the centre; if it comes out clean, it is ready.

COOL and serve slices topped with a dollop of coconut yoghurt.

Sugarless berry jelly

• SERVES 4–6 •

This is a luscious jelly full of all the good stuff. The natural sweetness and floral aromas of the berries are bright and bursting with flavour when not masked by the addition of sugar.

250 g (9 oz) frozen raspberries

$\frac{1}{2}$ teaspoon natural vanilla extract

2 tablespoons lemon juice

125 g ($4\frac{1}{2}$ oz) fresh raspberries

3 sheets gold-strength gelatine

125 g ($4\frac{1}{2}$ oz) fresh blueberries

125 g ($4\frac{1}{2}$ oz) strawberries, washed, hulled and thinly sliced

COMBINE the frozen raspberries, vanilla extract and lemon juice in a medium saucepan with 600 ml (21 fl oz) of water and bring to the boil.

REDUCE the heat and simmer for 8–10 minutes until the raspberries have broken down a little. Remove from the heat and allow the mixture to cool as the flavours infuse.

STRAIN through a fine sieve, but don't push the pulp through, as it will give the jelly a muddy colour. You should have approximately 500 ml (17 fl oz/2 cups) of raspberry liquid. If you have less, top it up with water.

SOAK the gelatine sheets in a bowl of cold water for 5 minutes to soften.

HEAT 250 ml (9 fl oz/1 cup) of the strained raspberry liquid to boiling point in a small saucepan, then remove from the heat. Gently squeeze the softened gelatine sheets to remove the excess water. Add the gelatine to the hot raspberry liquid and stir until dissolved. Then add the hot mixture to the remaining cold raspberry liquid and stand for 5 minutes to cool a little more.

SCATTER the fresh berries into a 1 litre (35 fl oz/4 cup) glass dish or jelly mould and gently pour the raspberry jelly mixture over the fruit.

SET in the fridge for at least 5 hours.

NOTE: There are different varieties of gelatine on the market. If you are not using the gold-strength sheets, follow the instructions on the packet and use the amount required for a soft hold with 500 ml (17 fl oz/2 cups) of liquid.

Banana, almond & date loaf

• SERVES 8–10 •

Even if you are dairy-, sugar- or gluten-intolerant, you will love this gorgeous moist loaf. It keeps for a week in a sealed container — if you hide it — but it's best refrigerated in hot weather.

---

285 g (10 oz) pitted dates, roughly chopped

$\frac{1}{2}$ teaspoon bicarbonate of soda (baking soda)

125 ml (4 fl oz/$\frac{1}{2}$ cup) extra virgin coconut oil

1 teaspoon ground cinnamon

3 bananas, approximately 300 g (10$\frac{1}{2}$ oz) when peeled

2 eggs

80 ml (2$\frac{1}{2}$ fl oz/$\frac{1}{3}$ cup) orange juice

150 g (5$\frac{1}{2}$ oz/1$\frac{1}{2}$ cups) almond meal

55 g (2 oz/$\frac{3}{4}$ cup) shredded coconut

1 teaspoon baking powder

160 g (5$\frac{3}{4}$ oz/1 cup) whole almonds, roughly chopped

PREHEAT the oven to 160°C (315°F). Line a 23 cm (9 inch) loaf (bar) tin with baking paper (I always grease the tin first so the paper sticks better).

PUT 185 g (6$\frac{1}{2}$ oz) of the dates, 185 ml (6 fl oz/$\frac{3}{4}$ cup) of water and the bicarbonate of soda in a small saucepan and bring to the boil, then reduce the heat and simmer over low heat for about 5 minutes, or until the dates break down. Remove from the heat and allow to cool.

BLITZ the coconut oil, cinnamon, cooled dates and bananas in a food processor until light and creamy.

ADD the eggs and orange juice, then blitz until smooth.

ADD the almond meal, shredded coconut and baking powder and pulse to just combine.

FOLD in half of the remaining dates and half of the chopped almonds.

POUR into the prepared loaf tin and scatter with the remaining chopped almonds and dates.

BAKE for 55–65 minutes until a skewer inserted into the centre comes out clean, keeping in mind that it's a very moist loaf.

Banana, chia & almond cupcakes *with* honeyed labneh

• MAKES ABOUT 16 •

This is the most delicious and moist cupcake mix inspired by my gorgeous baking friend, Rix. It's gluten free and a wonderful treat for any special occasion.

---

550 g (1 lb 4 oz) banana flesh (about 5–6 bananas, peeled)

8 eggs

200 g (7 oz) caster (superfine) sugar

1 teaspoon natural vanilla extract

375 g (13 oz/3¾ cups) almond meal

2 tablespoons chia seeds

2 teaspoons baking powder, sifted

PREHEAT a fan-forced oven to 160°C (315°F) or a regular oven to 180°C (350°F).

BLITZ the banana flesh, eggs, sugar and vanilla together in a food processor until smooth.

ADD the almond meal, chia seeds and baking powder to the mixture in the food processor. Pulse gently a few times to just combine.

POUR the mixture into straight-sided cupcake cases or moulds, filling each one three-quarters full.

BAKE for 25–30 minutes until golden on top. Insert a skewer into the centre of a cake and, if it comes out clean, the cakes are ready.

COOL and fill with honeyed labneh (see recipe below). Add a swirl of labneh to the top and decorate with edible flowers.

HONEYED LABNEH

500 g (1 lb 2 oz) plain yoghurt

1 heaped tablespoon honey

½ teaspoon vanilla bean paste

HONEYED LABNEH

STRAIN the yoghurt overnight through a fine mesh sieve or muslin (cheesecloth) set over a bowl in the fridge to release the whey (liquid).

DISCARD the whey and combine the strained yoghurt, honey and vanilla bean paste together in a bowl.

STIR until smooth. The mixture should be the consistency of whipped cream.

SPOON or use a piping (icing) bag to apply a generous amount of labneh on top of each cupcake.

Yummy apple cake

• SERVES 8–10 •

For this cake I precook the apple in golden syrup and butter, which makes it delicious,
but perhaps in some people's eyes a little naughty. I'm keeping it in the 'nice' section
because it's made of fresh, whole ingredients.

---

7 granny smith apples, peeled
   and cored

175 g (6 oz/$\frac{1}{2}$ cup) golden syrup
   (light treacle)

200 g (7 oz) butter, diced,
   at room temperature

385 g (13$\frac{1}{2}$ oz/1$\frac{3}{4}$ cups) caster
   (superfine) sugar

125 ml (4 fl oz/$\frac{1}{2}$ cup) grapeseed oil

finely grated zest of 1 lemon

1 teaspoon ground cinnamon

$\frac{1}{2}$ teaspoon natural vanilla extract

3 eggs

450 g (1 lb/3 cups) self-raising flour

250 ml (9 fl oz/1 cup) milk

1 tablespoon sugar, for sprinkling

a pinch of ground cinnamon,
   for sprinkling

PREHEAT a fan-forced oven to 160°C (315°F) or a regular oven to 180°C (350°F). Line a 23 cm (9 inch) round cake tin with baking paper.

CUT the apples into quarters and then cut each quarter in half again.

HEAT the golden syrup with half the butter in a medium saucepan over low heat for a few minutes until well combined and starting to bubble.

ADD the apple pieces to the saucepan, increase the heat to medium–high and cook for 8–10 minutes until the apples are golden in colour and half-cooked. Stir occasionally so they don't stick. Remove from the heat and set aside to cool slightly while you make the cake mixture.

BEAT the caster sugar, remaining butter, grapeseed oil, lemon zest, cinnamon and vanilla in the bowl of an electric mixer on high speed until really creamy.

ADD the eggs one at a time, continuing to beat until well combined.

SIFT in the flour, add the milk and fold it all together using a metal spoon until you have a smooth, light mixture.

SPOON half the cake mixture into the prepared cake tin and spread out evenly.

TOP with half of the cooked apple pieces and a few spoonfuls of the syrup. Repeat with the remaining cake mixture and apples. (If you have any syrup left, reserve it for pouring over the cake when it is fresh out of the oven.)

SPRINKLE the sugar and cinnamon over the top and bake for 50–60 minutes. Check whether the cake is cooked by inserting a skewer into the centre to make sure it comes out clean.

SERVE warm or cold with delicious double cream or ice cream.

Berry tarts *with* honeyed labneh cream

· MAKES 8 ·

I always make my own pastry and it's really worth the effort, but you can use ready-made frozen pastry to save time. Labneh has a wonderful creamy tang that works beautifully with the berries. I tried this recipe out on my husband and I think he momentarily loved me even more.

350 g (12 oz) plain yoghurt

1 tablespoon honey

$\frac{1}{4}$ teaspoon vanilla bean paste

1 quantity sweet shortcrust pastry (see recipe below), or use 3 sheets of ready-made shortcrust pastry

100 ml ($3\frac{1}{2}$ fl oz) thin (pouring) cream, whipped to soft peaks

125 g ($4\frac{1}{2}$ oz) raspberries

125 g ($4\frac{1}{2}$ oz) blueberries

125 g ($4\frac{1}{2}$ oz) boysenberries (optional)

125 g ($4\frac{1}{2}$ oz) strawberries

STRAIN the yoghurt overnight through a fine mesh sieve or muslin (cheesecloth) set over a bowl in the fridge to release the whey (liquid). Discard the whey and combine the strained yoghurt, honey and vanilla bean paste together in a bowl. Stir until smooth. Refrigerate.

ROLL the pastry between two sheets of plastic wrap until it is about 4 mm ($\frac{1}{8}$ inch) thick. Cut out eight 10 cm (4 inch) rounds. Press the rounds into lightly greased 8 cm ($3\frac{1}{4}$ inch) round fluted loose-based tart tins. Trim off the excess pastry around the top and prick each base all over using a fork. Rest for 30 minutes in the fridge.

PREHEAT a fan-forced oven to 170°C (325°F) or a regular oven to 190°C (375°F).

COVER the pastry cases with baking paper and fill with pastry weights, dried beans or rice. Blind bake for 10–15 minutes until firm. Remove the weights and baking paper and bake uncovered for a further 5–10 minutes until golden and crispy. Allow to cool.

STIR the honeyed labneh and whipped cream together until smooth. Scoop a generous spoonful of honeyed labneh cream mixture into each of the cooled tart cases.

TOP with fresh berries. Eat immediately or store in the fridge until ready to devour.

SWEET SHORTCRUST PASTRY

Makes 1 large tart base or 8 small ones

180 g ($6\frac{1}{4}$ oz) plain (all-purpose) flour

75 g ($2\frac{3}{4}$ oz) icing (confectioners') sugar

100 g ($3\frac{1}{2}$ oz) unsalted butter, diced

2 egg yolks, lightly beaten with a fork

1 teaspoon water

$\frac{1}{2}$ teaspoon natural vanilla extract

SWEET SHORTCRUST PASTRY

PROCESS the flour, icing sugar and butter in a food processor until it resembles breadcrumbs.

WHISK the egg yolks, water and vanilla extract together in a small bowl, then add to the mixture in the food processor and pulse three or four times until combined.

TURN the pastry onto a clean work surface and gently push it together with your hands to form a ball.

WRAP it in plastic wrap and put it in the fridge to rest for 30 minutes before rolling it out.

Baked stone fruit

• SERVES 6–8 •

Come summer and autumn, in the peak of stone fruit season, the price comes down and the fruit tastes best. For a dinner party, or just to spoil my family, I like to bake them in the oven, sprinkled with a few tasty ingredients and a bit of love, which intensifies the beautiful flavours.

12 stone fruits (such as nectarines, peaches and plums)

2 tablespoons maple syrup

2 tablespoons sugar

1 teaspoon ground cinnamon

plain yoghurt, whipped cream or thick (double) cream, to serve

PREHEAT a fan-forced oven to 180°C (350°F) or a regular oven to 200°C (400°F). Line a baking tin with baking paper.

CUT the fruit in half at the equator and take out the stones. (You can remove the stones after baking if they don't come out easily!)

PLACE the fruit in the prepared tin, skin side down, drizzle with maple syrup then sprinkle with sugar and cinnamon.

BAKE for 20–25 minutes.

REMOVE from the oven, turn the fruit over to soak up the juice, and allow to cool.

STORE in a glass container with any residual juices in the fridge. The fruit will keep for several days.

SERVE with plain yoghurt, whipped cream or thick cream.

DELICIOUS for breakfast with yoghurt and muesli.

Sweet and NAUGHTY

Diet is the new religion, therefore sacrifices must be made. With all the bad news and naysaying about sugar and flour, it's hard to be a believer in dessert, but I am stubborn when it comes to the things I love.

When I'm told not to do something, it makes me want to break all the rules. Don't jump into the pool! Don't run! Eat with your mouth shut! Use a knife and fork! Sit up straight! Sound familiar? Well, I am having dessert and you can't stop me. Join me if you dare.

Chocolate date nut torte

This gorgeous torte is the hybrid of a pavlova and a panforte. This is the kind of dessert that even non-dessert-eaters can't resist.

---

250 g (9 oz) pitted dates

250 g (9 oz) dark chocolate buttons

250 g (9 oz) almonds

6 egg whites

150 g (5½ oz/⅔ cup) caster
(superfine) sugar

300 ml (10½ fl oz) cream, whipped
unsweetened cocoa powder, for dusting

PREHEAT a fan-forced oven to 160°C (315°F) or a regular oven to 180°C (350°F). Line a 23 cm (9 inch) round cake tin with baking paper.

SLICE each date into about 4 pieces.

PULSE the chocolate buttons and almonds in a food processor with a blade attachment for 3-second intervals until roughly chopped (a similar size to the sliced dates).

COMBINE the chocolate, dates and almonds together in a large bowl.

BEAT the egg whites until stiff and gradually add the sugar. Continue to beat until well combined and glossy.

FOLD the egg whites gently into the chocolate mixture.

SPOON evenly into the prepared cake tin.

BAKE for 40 minutes, or until lightly golden and crunchy on the outside. Remove and cool completely in the tin.

SERVE topped with the whipped cream and dusted with sifted cocoa.

Mexican spiced chocolate cake

• SERVES 12–16 • GANACHE MAKES 1 CUP (ABOUT 350 G/12 OZ) •

The great thing about a flourless chocolate cake is that you can make it well in advance because it has a great shelf life. You can dress it up with a chocolate ganache or serve it simply dusted with cocoa, cinnamon and icing sugar. I think the Mexican spices give this cake a little extra magic.

180 g (6¼ oz) butter, at room temperature

180 g (6¼ oz) dark chocolate buttons

½ teaspoon ground allspice

1 teaspoon ground cinnamon, plus extra, for dusting (optional)

½ teaspoon ground chilli

5 eggs, separated

125 g (4½ oz) caster (superfine) sugar

180 g (6¼ oz) almond meal

1 tablespoon unsweetened cocoa powder or ground coffee beans

½ teaspoon baking powder

3 teaspoons unsweetened cocoa powder, extra, for dusting (optional)

2 teaspoons icing (confectioners') sugar, for dusting (optional)

PREHEAT a fan-forced oven to 160°C (315°F) or a regular oven to 180°C (350°F). Line a greased 23 cm (9 inch) round cake tin with baking paper.

MELT the butter, chocolate, spices and chilli together in the top of a double-boiler until smooth and well combined. Allow to cool slightly.

BEAT the egg yolks and caster sugar until pale and creamy.

SLOWLY add the chocolate mixture to the egg yolk mixture while continuing to beat.

FOLD in the almond meal and sift in the cocoa powder (or coffee) and baking powder. Set aside.

BEAT the egg whites until soft peaks form. Fold half of the beaten whites into the chocolate mixture to loosen it, then gently fold in the remaining whites until just combined.

POUR the batter into the prepared cake tin.

BAKE for about 40 minutes. This is a moist cake so, when tested with a skewer inserted into the centre, the skewer should be a little bit sticky when it comes out.

COOL the cake and cover with ganache (see recipe below) or alternatively combine the extra cocoa, icing sugar and extra ground cinnamon in a sieve and dust over the cake.

SALTY TOFFEE CHOCOLATE GANACHE

55 g (2 oz/¼ cup) caster (superfine) sugar

100 ml (3½ fl oz) thin (pouring) cream

20 g (¾ oz) butter, diced, at room temperature

¼ teaspoon sea salt

200 g (7 oz) dark cooking chocolate, blitzed in a food processor to fine meal

dried chilli flakes and sea salt, to garnish

SALTY TOFFEE CHOCOLATE GANACHE

HEAT the sugar and 30 ml (1 fl oz) of water in a small heavy-based saucepan over high heat for 3–5 minutes until it turns a dark golden toffee colour. Watch it carefully to avoid burning but don't stir it!

REMOVE from the heat and immediately pour in the cream and butter while whisking vigorously until combined.

WHISK in the salt and chocolate until smooth and shiny.

COOL in the saucepan for about 10 minutes so it sets slightly.

SPOON the ganache over the cake and smooth with a spatula, allowing the ganache to drip down the sides.

SPRINKLE with chilli flakes and a little more sea salt to serve.

Pear & pecan upside-down tart

· SERVES 6–8 ·

I have been making upside-down tarts since I was a little girl. Not only are they delicious, but they have great wow factor, especially when you turn them out at the table in front of your family or friends. This recipe also works well with other fruits, such as apples, plums, apricots and peaches.

---

60 ml (2 fl oz/¼ cup) maple syrup

2 tablespoons dark brown sugar

40 g (1½ oz) butter

a pinch of ground ginger

1 kg (2 lb 4 oz) pears, peeled, quartered and cored

1 lemon, for squeezing

50 g (1¾ oz/½ cup) pecan nuts

2 sheets frozen puff pastry, partially thawed, or sweet shortcrust pastry (see page 188)

double (thick) cream, ice cream or yoghurt, to serve

PREHEAT a fan-forced oven to 180°C (350°F) or a regular oven to 200 (400°F).

MELT the maple syrup and brown sugar in a 25 cm (10 inch) ovenproof frying pan until the sugar dissolves and the mixture starts to bubble.

ADD the butter and ginger and cook for a few more minutes over medium to low heat. Keep stirring with a wooden spoon for about 2 minutes until the mixture starts to caramelise.

ADD the pears and a squeeze of lemon juice to the pan and cook over medium heat for a few minutes, tossing the pears to coat them in the syrup.

COVER with a lid, reduce the heat and simmer for 10–12 minutes until the pears soften a little.

UNCOVER and add the pecans, then turn the heat up to high. Cook for a further 3 minutes, coating pears and pecans generously in the syrup. Stir to prevent the caramel from burning until the syrup is reduced to a thick consistency.

REMOVE the pan from the heat and allow to cool.

JOIN 2 sheets of pastry together by cutting each sheet in half on the diagonal. Join the 4 triangles together with the corners in the centre to make one big square.

LAY the pastry over the pears in the pan. Tuck the overhanging edges of the pastry into the pan.

PIERCE the pastry in a few places with a skewer or fork.

BAKE for 30 minutes, or until the pastry is golden brown.

REST for 5 minutes and run a knife around the edges before placing a serving plate or platter on top and, quickly and confidently, turning the tart out.

SERVE warm with double cream, ice cream or yoghurt.

DELICIOUS served warm or cold as leftovers the next day.

The 'Breaking Bad' flan

The first time I ate a good custard flan was in Albuquerque, New Mexico. Because I'm a caramel custard lover, it's hard to forget such a treat. I made up this recipe based on that flavour memory and named it in honour of that iconic TV series from the same city — it's equally naughty and just as addictive!

220 g (7¾ oz/1 cup) white sugar

finely grated zest of 1 orange

1 x 270 ml (9½ fl oz) tin coconut cream

1 x 395 g (13¾ oz) tin sweetened condensed milk

300 ml (10½ fl oz) thin (pouring) cream

3 eggs

3 egg yolks, extra

1 tablespoon sugar, extra

½ teaspoon natural vanilla extract

PREHEAT a fan-forced oven to 140°C (275°F) or a regular oven to 160°C (315°F).

COMBINE the sugar and 3 tablespoons of water in a heavy-based saucepan over low heat. Stir just until the sugar dissolves.

ADD the orange zest and gently simmer without stirring over medium heat for 7–10 minutes until the syrup turns a deep golden caramel colour.

REMOVE immediately from the heat and carefully pour the caramel evenly over the base of a 1 litre (35 fl oz/4 cup) flan dish. Allow to cool and set.

HEAT the coconut cream, condensed milk and cream in a small saucepan over low heat. Stir to prevent the condensed milk from burning and remove from heat just before boiling.

BEAT the eggs, egg yolks, extra sugar and vanilla extract together in a stainless-steel bowl until the mixture is creamy.

POUR in the heated coconut cream mixture slowly while constantly whisking until smooth.

POUR the mixture through a fine sieve over the cooled caramel syrup in the flan dish.

LINE a roasting tin with a damp tea towel (dish towel). Place the flan dish on top and pour in enough boiling water around the outside of the flan dish to reach halfway up the side.

BAKE uncovered, for 30–40 minutes until the centre of the flan is set but still wobbly.

REMOVE from the oven and allow to cool. Refrigerate for at least 5 hours, but for best results make it the day before you turn it out.

RUN a small knife around the edge of the flan for easy release. Place a large platter with a rim over the top, flip the whole thing over, and gently remove the flan dish to reveal the upside-down flan topped with oozing caramel.

DELICIOUS served with an extra dollop of cream.

Fruity pie

· SERVES 8–10 ·

You have to love a pie when you don't have to roll any pastry. This works well with any fruit, but is extra delicious with baked stone fruit (see page 190). It also works well with gluten-free flour.

flour, for dusting flan dish

250 g (9 oz) butter, cubed,
   at room temperature

200 g (7 oz) caster (superfine) sugar

3 eggs

250 g (9 oz/1½ cups) almond meal

3 tablespoons self-raising flour

2 cups stewed or baked stone fruit

2–3 tablespoons flaked almonds

icing (confectioners') sugar, for dusting
   (optional)

PREHEAT a fan-forced oven to 160°C (315°F) or a regular oven to 180°C (350°F). Grease a 25 cm (10 inch) long, 4 cm (1½ inch) high oval ceramic flan dish and dust with flour.

BEAT the butter and caster sugar until light and creamy.

ADD the eggs one at a time while still beating.

ADD the almond meal and self-raising flour and mix to just combine.

SPREAD two-thirds of the mixture over the base of the prepared flan dish.

ARRANGE the fruit over the top, leaving a 2 cm (¾ inch) strip uncovered around the edge.

SPOON dollops of the remaining mixture over and between fruit. It might not look like enough but it will rise and spread.

SCATTER with the flaked almonds.

BAKE for 45–50 minutes until golden.

SERVE dusted with icing sugar (if using).

DELICIOUS with cream or ice cream.

Panna cotta *with* cardamom-spiced pink grapefruit

I always feel like I'm cheating when I make this dessert: it's really simple to whip up and so easy to scoff down. The only time-consuming part is the setting period. It's a great dessert to make ahead of time if you are having a fancy dinner party or just want to spoil your family.

½ vanilla bean, halved lengthways

250 ml (9 fl oz/1 cup) thin (pouring) cream

250 ml (9 fl oz/1 cup) milk

55 g (2 oz/¼ cup) caster (superfine) sugar

2 sheets gold-strength gelatine

SCRAPE the vanilla seeds into a medium saucepan and add the cream, milk, sugar and the vanilla pod.

SIMMER over low heat for 5–6 minutes to infuse the flavours and dissolve the sugar. Do not boil. Remove from the heat and allow the flavours to infuse for a few more minutes. Discard the vanilla pod.

MEANWHILE, soak the gelatine in cold water for 5 minutes then squeeze out the excess water and gently whisk the gelatine into the warm cream mixture until dissolved.

TRANSFER to a glass bowl and set it over a bowl of iced water. Allow to stand for approximately 20 minutes, gently whisking occasionally until the mixture cools, slightly thickens and the vanilla seeds are suspended.

TRANSFER to a jug and carefully pour the mixture into small dessert glasses until they are three-quarters full. Refrigerate for about 4 hours until set.

SERVE topped with spiced pink grapefruit (see recipe below). It's also delicious with saffron pears in cider (see page 206) or baked stone fruit (see page 190).

SPICED PINK GRAPEFRUIT

2 pink grapefruit

110 g (3¾ oz/½ cup) sugar

2 cardamom pods, crushed

1 cinnamon stick

a capful of Cointreau (orange–flavoured liqueur)

SPICED PINK GRAPEFRUIT

PEEL and segment the grapefruit. Set aside the segments and squeeze the empty skins of the grapefruit over a bowl to capture the juice. You should get about 125 ml (4 fl oz/½ cup). Reserve the juice.

HEAT the sugar with 125 ml (4 fl oz/½ cup) of water and the spices in a small saucepan over medium heat for about 10 minutes, until reduced to a syrupy consistency.

ADD the reserved grapefruit juice and the liqueur and cook for a further minute. Remove from the heat, allow to cool, then strain.

ADD the grapefruit segments to the cooled syrup.

Saffron pears in cider

· SERVES 6 ·

This is a stunning dinner party dessert. You can make it well in advance as it keeps for up to a week in the fridge. The combination of the cider and saffron gives it a unique and delicious flavour without being too sweet.

100 g (3½ oz/½ cup lightly packed) light brown sugar

1 litre (35 fl oz/4 cups) apple and pear cider

1 teaspoon saffron threads

1 cinnamon stick

1 vanilla bean, split lengthways

finely grated zest and juice of 2 oranges

6 pears, peeled and cores removed through the base

PUT the sugar, cider, saffron, cinnamon stick, vanilla bean, orange zest and juice in a 3 litre (105 fl oz/12 cup) saucepan and bring to the boil.

ADD the pears and gently simmer for 10–20 minutes until still firm but easily skewered. Cooking time will depend on the size and ripeness of pears.

REMOVE the pears with a slotted spoon, transfer to a bowl, then cover and set aside.

REDUCE the syrup by two-thirds over medium heat.

POUR the reduced syrup over the pears and allow to cool.

SERVE in a bowl or fanned out on a plate with lots of syrup.

DELICIOUS with vanilla bean ice cream, double (thick) cream, crème fraîche, coconut yoghurt or panna cotta (see page 204).

Index

Acknowledgements

Firstly I would like to thank my two amazing friends — food stylist Ursula Nairn and cake queen Rix McCormack — for helping me with this book from the very beginning to the end. This book would not have been possible without you both.

FAMILY AND FRIENDS
My husband, Luc, for all his help, love and support.

My mum and dad, and Sophie and Ben Elton for their generosity.

My brother-in-law, Griffin Longley, for his creative input. My mother-in-law, Sue Hansen, for the first edit of the recipes. My loyal friend Tania King who over many cups of tea (and wine) crossed my T's and dotted my I's.

Pauline Tresise, Bec Obrien, Lily, Clare, Jackson and Elsie for helping out and doing loads of dishes. Fiona Whittles, Bridget Norton and Holly Bodeker-Smith for their words of wisdom.

MANAGEMENT
Bridget Lorimer and Justine May at *Chefs*INK for managing me, and Andrew Taylor for years gone by.

MURDOCH BOOKS
All the amazing and talented crew at Murdoch for making fabulous cookbooks: Jane Morrow (publisher), Katie Bosher (editorial manager) and Megan Pigott (design manager).

Melody Lord (editor) Christine Osmond (food editor), Christine Farmer (publicist) and Alissa Dinallo for the beautiful design on *Delicious Every Day*.

SHOOTING THE BOOK
A big thanks to Craig Kinder for the beautiful photographs and Emma Van Dordrecht at f22 photography

Also to James Campbell and Kelly Davies (photography assistants), Ursula Nairn (food stylist) and Rix McCormack (home economist) for all their hard work.

Sydney cover shoot: Thanks to Rob Palmer (photographer), Vanessa Austin (stylist) and Jo Cotter (hair and makeup) for their work on the cover.

A special thank you to the Boatshed Market in Cottesloe for supplying us with all the beautiful produce for this book.

Published in 2016 by Murdoch Books, an imprint of Allen & Unwin
Murdoch Books Australia
83 Alexander Street
Crows Nest NSW 2065
Phone: +61 (0) 2 8425 0100
Fax: +61 (0) 2 9906 2218
murdochbooks.com.au
info@murdochbooks.com.au

Murdoch Books UK
Ormond House
26–27 Boswell Street
London WC1N 3JZ
Phone: +44 (0) 20 8785 5995
murdochbooks.co.uk
info@murdochbooks.co.uk

For Corporate Orders & Custom Publishing, contact our
Business Development Team at salesenquiries@murdochbooks.com.au.

Publisher: Jane Morrow
Editorial Manager: Katie Bosher
Design Manager: Megan Pigott
Project Editor: Melody Lord
Designer and illustrator: Alissa Dinallo
Photographer: Craig Kinder
Stylist: Ursula Nann
Cover Stylist: Vanessa Austin
Food Editor: Christine Osmond
Home Economist: Rix McCormack
Production Manager: Alexandra Gonzalez

A cataloguing-in-publication entry is available from the catalogue of the National Library
of Australia at nla.gov.au.

ISBN 978 1 74266 390 6 Australia
ISBN 978 1 74336 741 4 UK

A catalogue record for this book is available from the British Library.

Colour reproduction by Splitting Image Colour Studio Pty Ltd, Clayton, Victoria
Printed by 1010 Printing International Limited, China

IMPORTANT: Those who might be at risk from the effects of salmonella poisoning (the
elderly, pregnant women, young children and those suffering from immune deficiency
diseases) should consult their doctor with any concerns about eating raw eggs.

OVEN GUIDE: You may find cooking times vary depending on the oven you are using.
For fan-forced ovens, as a general rule, set the oven temperature to 20°C (35°F) lower than
indicated in the recipe.

MEASURES GUIDE: We have used 20 ml (4 teaspoon) tablespoon measures. If you are
using a 15 ml (3 teaspoon) tablespoon add an extra teaspoon of the ingredient for each
tablespoon specified.